SONG MAPS

A NEW SYSTEM TO WRITE YOUR BEST LYRICS

SIMON HAWKINS

Published by Great British Book Publishing, London

GET YOUR FREE WORKBOOK!

I've found that readers have the most success implementing Song Maps when they have the opportunity to work through some real-life exercises and examples of putting the principles in the book into practice.

So, to say thank you for purchasing *Song Maps – A New System to Write Your Best Lyrics*, I'd like to give you the Workbook for free!

http://bit.ly/SongMapWorkbook

To my beautiful, super-talented wife, Sandra.

To God, Author of all.

To all who carry a deep hunger to excel in their craft for His glory.

CONTENTS

INTRODUCTION

Welcome to the second edition of *Song Maps – A New System to Write Your Best Lyrics!*

I just wanted to say a few words on what's happened to this book over the last four years.

When you write your first book, you never quite know what impact it might have. Specifically, you never know until it's out there whether it's going to be something others might find interesting. And until the book was published in May 2016, I was still a little nervous.

However, this book has been on a fantastic journey; it has achieved:

- Amazon's #1 Best Seller many weeks, even today
- Sales in 13 countries
- Opportunities to teach this internationally

- A stream of emails from my lovely readers, connecting, asking questions, and,
- So many people have found it helpful on their own songwriting journey

Thank you to all my readers for making this a wonderful experience.

As I write this introduction, my next book, *The Organized Songwriter – How to Create Space to Write Your Best Songs,* will be published in about a week. I have the same nerves I had with Song Maps, but I hope it will be an incredible journey for you to read as it was for this book.

This second edition is similar to the original edition, only updated for a few things and formatted to look more like the new book. I hope and pray this that God blesses your writing. As I say at the end of this book: you have an extraordinary journey ahead of you. Enjoy!

– SJLH.

1 INTRO

It has never been harder to make an impact as a songwriter. To survive, let alone be recognized and win awards, your craft has to be the best it can be. And then some

Whether you're just starting out as a songwriter, you're an experienced songwriter or just looking for a new perspective on the beautiful craft of songwriting, this book offers fresh insights to help you write your very best lyrics.

Does any of the following sound familiar?

- You worry that the lyrics you write just don't deliver their full potential but can't figure out why, even though technically they tick all the right boxes.
- You have great ideas but your finished lyrics somehow fall short of the emotional impact you wanted and, as a result, your songs get passed over.
- You have a busy schedule with limited time to write

and have wasted too many hours chasing unwritable lyric ideas.
- You wonder how some professional songwriters always seem to get a particular dynamic in their lyrics, consistently writing songs better than 90% of what you hear on the radio.
- You are perhaps nervous about going into a pro co-writing session because you fear your ideas aren't worth bringing into the writing room.
- You know you have so many great titles waiting to be written but haven't found a way of systematically developing them into well-crafted lyrics.
- After writing an amazing hooky Chorus and a great supporting first Verse, you hit the dreaded wall that is s-e-c-o-n-d v-e-r-s-e c-u-r-s-e.

In Song Maps – A New System to Write Your Best Lyrics I deliver simple, logical, well-defined solutions to these issues and more: I give you seven well-developed professional templates for you to bring your lyrics to life. I also provide you with a tried and tested process for writing lyrics using Song Maps. And I'll reveal the songwriter's secret weapon.

Much of this book contains new material. This is because, while I enjoyed building a firm foundation of knowledge about the craft from the songwriting programs at Berklee Music School and other sources, I discovered Song Maps afterward, from my experience as a professional songwriter, writing either on my own or in the writing rooms of Nashville.

This book is for those who are tired of writing ideas that, despite being good in concept, end up being flat when finally written. Or those who find it difficult to know how to develop their songs to give them the emotional punch they originally had in mind when they first had the idea. It's for those searching hard for that elusive "aha" moment when trying to develop their lyric writing craft to pro-standard, rather than wasting years trying to work it out by themselves.

Having been signed as a staff songwriter at Universal Music Publishing in Nashville, being nominated and winning awards for my songs including Grammys, Doves and hymn-writing awards, and after spending many years studying thousands of techniques and developing them in my own songwriting and in the writing room, I've had the privilege of teaching the material in this book to hundreds of songwriters and seeing a step change in their writing. I have been blessed to watch them find their authentic voice in writing ideas to their full potential, helping them achieve their dream to move from writing flat 2D lyrics to fabulous High Definition full-color 3D lyrics.

Known by many as the guy who teaches lyric strategies, I've explored and analyzed thousands of song lyrics in many genres, studying what makes them work and what lets them down. I've also critiqued hundreds of lyrics given to me by students of songwriting.

Through the lessons in this book, you'll gain a whole new set of tools that will help you simply and swiftly deal with the ups and downs of writing lyrics so they will deliver the emotional punch you are looking for, tools that will make your songs stand out in the marketplace and help you achieve your potential and calling as a songwriter.

Whether you're looking to better manage the idea flow of your lyrics, increase your bank of writable ideas, walk into a pro co-write with confidence or look at your lyrics afresh and make them...

***** SHINE *****

...you will find this book essential reading.

Sue C Smith, five-time Dove-award winning songwriter, staff writer with Capitol CMG and founder of the Write About Jesus seminar for Christian songwriters, says:

> "Simon Hawkins is a gifted problem-solver, and so much of songwriting calls for just that. In Song Maps – A New System To Write Your Best Lyrics, Simon has shared the methods he has developed to catapult his own songwriting career and offered them to songwriters everywhere. It's going to revolutionize and illuminate the process for so many. What a wonderful, generous gift to the songwriting community!"
>
> SUE C SMITH

Let this book help you transform your lyric writing by using Song Maps in your songwriting workflow and take your song ideas to their ultimate potential. Find out how you might be compromising the quality of your lyric writing by not seeing the full range of possibilities. Take action to quickly screen out un-writable ideas, the titles that suck your time away from writing your best, truly golden, spectacular songs.

Andrea Stolpe, instructor at Berklee Music School, multi-platinum recorded songwriter, artist and author says:

> "Simon offers songwriters creative parameters where so many claim no parameters can be set. With such tangible tools, songwriters can experience great freedom and expect consistent results."
>
> ANDREA STOLPE

As you read on, you'll hear about how I discovered how to shift from writing what I call "2D lyrics" to crafting fabulous, dynamic "3D lyrics"; about the songwriter's secret weapon; about the difference between a title and a writable idea; about why the flow of ideas is important within your lyrics; and a foolproof four-step process for writing with Song Maps.

I'll share with you specific steps that will help you transform your writing workflow.

When you take the time to develop your craft, there is a vast body of knowledge that makes up the technical side of the craft, which you need to have before you can shape your songs to their full potential.

Pat Pattison, Professor of Lyric Writing and Poetry at Berklee College of Music, said it best:

> "Much of lyric writing is technical. The stronger your skills are, the better you can express your creative ideas."
>
> PAT PATTISON

And Pat is right–it's up to each one of us to decide how much we're willing to invest in our own craft, to be students long enough to achieve our full potential as writers.

Song Maps – A New System to Write Your Best Lyrics sets out clear, actionable steps for identifying the potential of a title before you even think about rhyme schemes and melodies. As you assimilate Song Maps into your writing workflow, your songwriting will shift away from tentative, self-conscious, inhibited writing to strong, bold, intentional and vulnerable writing that does full justice to your original ideas, ultimately allowing you to make the impact you deserve as a songwriter.

If you implement the simple, easy-to-understand concepts in this book, I promise you your songs will be better crafted than 90% of the songs you hear on the radio. It will also transform your effectiveness as a co-writer. Importantly, no matter where your songs end up, you will be confident you have written a brilliant lyric and you have served your co-writers well.

Ultimately this book will give you practical steps to become the writer you are called to be. But you must implement these concepts and follow through with practice.

As legendary speaker and author Anthony Robbins said:

> "A real decision is measured by the fact that you've taken a new action. If there's no action, you haven't truly decided."
>
> ANTHONY ROBBINS

It's time to stop settling for second-best in your lyric writing. It's time to move your craft to the next level, for the amazing ideas you have for your songs to be crafted to their full potential. It's time to achieve your ultimate goals as a writer–not just for yourself, but for all those who sing and hear your songs. It's time for your song ideas to get out there and be heard, because they were given to you for a reason.

All you need to do is keep reading to learn the benefits of writing with Song Maps, how they can be an essential part of your writing process and what you can do to save yourself and your co-writers the heartache of having your songs continually rejected and to celebrate the joy of writing every idea to its very best.

Discover this new technique for your writing and use it to transform your old approach to lyric writing to write your best lyrics and achieve your calling as a songwriter.

Read on. Be inspired. And be moved by what you will find yourself writing.

Overview

Before we begin your new journey with Song Mapping, let's take a look at what exactly we'll be covering. I've split this book into several parts:

- Chapter 1 – **Intro** (here!)
- Chapter 2 – **Five reasons** for using Song Maps, including the idea of writing in 3D rather than in 2D, how to protect your creative time, the full potential of developing a title, how to prepare for co-writes and, maybe the most important part, how to banish Second Verse Curse.
- Chapter 3 – **What is Song Mapping**, including the principle of honoring the idea, plot versus story, why the flow of ideas is key for songwriters, the

songwriter's secret weapon, and the idea of writable ideas.

- Chapter 4 – **How to Use Song Maps**, the four-step process for writing with Maps, how to write literally *any* title, and how to use Song Maps in the writing room.
- Chapter 5 – **Seven universal Song Maps** is where I introduce the main meat of this book: Tension/Response, Problem/Declaration, Timezones, Places, Roles, Twist, and Literal/Figurative. In each, I show how it works and examples of these in practice in the commercial world.
- Chapter 6 – **What next?**, is where to learn how to find more Song Maps, how to combine Maps together, the way you can alter Song Maps, and how it can work in different song forms. Finally, I introduce the idea of Advanced Song Mapping.
- Chapter 7 – an **Outro**, where I show how to write an impossible title, where to start using Song Maps, and finally, some final comments.

The Organized Songwriter

If you want to hear more about my second book, *The Organized Songwriter – How to Create Space to Write Your Best Songs* – you can find out more about this in my book at Amazon as well as the accompanying Workbook, *The Organized Songwriter Workbook.*

The
Organized
Songwriter
How to Create Space to
Write Your Best Songs
SIMON HAWKINS

2 FIVE REASONS TO USE SONG MAPS

Since discovering Song Maps some twelve years ago, I have built up a bank of around 500 writable ideas that travel with me everywhere. They have been instrumental in writing #1 hit songs, Grammy-nominated songs, Dove-nominated musicals and the Hymn of 2015.

They have also helped me:

- Transform my lyric writing from flat, 2D lyrics to glorious 3D full-color lyrics
- Saved me precious creative time during a busy schedule
- Enabled me to look at titles in totally new ways
- Helped me serve my co-writers better in the writing room, and
- Completely banish "Second Verse Curse"

In short, they transformed the way I write songs and the way I feel about writing, eliminating many of the frustrating, stressful, random elements that can often sabotage a writing session.

In this chapter, I'll briefly run through how these benefits can transform your writing before discussing in later chapters what Song Maps are in detail, how to use them in your writing and offer seven universal Song Maps that you can immediately use in your own writing.

While I often talk about songwriting in the context of co-writing, all of the ideas and principles in this book are totally applicable, in fact I'd say even more applicable, to writing solo.

A little planning goes a long, long way

As songwriters, we love to spend time in our right brains, where we can be artistic, creative, imaginative, intuitive, emotional, spatial. Some songwriters I know love it so much that I won't even schedule a co-write with them because I know from experience they're too creative to even turn up for the co-write!

But for anyone willing to embrace a little more left-brain processing, applying a little bit of planning to our writing goes a long, long way. In fact, I'd even suggest it's the most logical thing to do.

- Do we have a plan for how we spend money?

- Do we have a plan for the rest of our day, week, year?
- Do we have savings for a rainy day?

Even if you can't say yes to all of these, wouldn't you agree that having a plan is better than not having a plan?

It's the same with your craft. God has blessed us with brains that process both reasoning and creativity. If we can use our whole brain to write songs, I believe we will write better songs. This is what Song Mapping is all about.

The big difference between using Song Maps and a simple lyric sketch is that, rather than leaving the direction of your lyric to chance, with Song Maps you write using predefined, tried and tested successful templates to develop the title, ensuring effective lyric development and providing you with a solid payoff.

In this chapter, I run through how I discovered Song Maps before setting out the top-five reasons why I continue to use them today, having made it an essential part of my own songwriting workflow.

How I discovered Song Maps

I discovered Song Maps out of desperation. When I was first signed as a staff songwriter to Universal Music Publishing in Nashville, I regularly traveled the 20-hour, 4,181-mile trip from my home in Felpham on the south coast of England to Cool Springs, Nashville to co-write with other staff writers and artists. I'd go five or six times a year, for a couple of weeks each time. While I was there, thanks to Holly Ward, my fabulous Creative Director, my calendar was often jammed with writing appointments–sometimes two or three a day.

Nashville is an extraordinary place in that it seems to operate on a totally different concept of time from the rest of the world–not Central Time, but what my wife and I often jokingly called "Nashville-stretchy-time." Let me just say that maybe 80% of the appointments on my calendar would actually happen.

It was, therefore, crucial for me to arrive in the writing room ready to serve my co-writers well. The most stupid thing in the world would be for me to go to all that trouble and hassle only to arrive in the writing room with no ideas. Or even worse, with half-baked, clichéd or sucky ideas. I, therefore, needed a consistent source of great, writable ideas and behind it a robust system to find them. The idea of Song Maps developed out of that.

What I didn't realize is how much Song Maps would transform my writing–whether I was writing on my own or with one of my 100 wonderful co-writers.

Having used this technique for a number of years now, there are so many good reasons to use Song Maps it's difficult to capture them all. Out of all the research and reading I have done on my journey as a songwriter, this approach has helped my writing the most.

The fact that Song Maps were something I developed on my own–rather than read in a book or found in a course–is the main reason I wanted to write this book: to share it with my fellow travelers and help them on their journey too.

Tools not rules

I often get asked,

"What's the best way to write a great song?"

Frankly, if standing on my head naked in a bucket of cold water would guarantee I would write a blockbuster hit every time, I would certainly do it. Even if it happened one in ten times, I'd probably still do it!

But life is not like that.

I'm sure you know already; there is no single right way to write a song. Not even in the writing rooms of Nashville, where hundreds of co-writers sit together each day and hammer out hit after hit; while the physical environment may look familiarly creative, and there are some unwritten conventions about how a co-write generally might unfold, these are certainly not hard-coded or written in stone. The only rule is that there are no rules and people just get on and write the best song they can. So it is in this spirit, of offering tools, not rules, that I write this. Let's now look at my top-five reasons for using Song Maps.

Reason 1 - To write in 3D rather than in 2D

When I realized the difference between writing in 2D and writing in 3D, it was a pivotal moment for my songwriting. By no means is it something all professional writers do, especially in genres that are not so lyric-driven–for example in Europe, where songs give less emphasis on lyrics but much more emphasis on groove, melody, and overall feel.

Many ways to write a title

Discovering how to write in 3D started when I finally got a writing appointment with one of my all-time songwriter heroes. I drove to their home in a lovely part of Nashville and settled down on their pristine sofa. As I sat there waiting for coffee to bubble through the machine, I surveyed their array of silver, gold and platinum records hanging on the wall in front of me, the performance area set up in the dining room, the flashing lights of the hardware studio enticing me to engage. Was I nervous? Yes. I was about to live out a bucket list moment.

They sat down next to me as we chatted over the industry, shared stories about our respective journeys and how the life of the songwriter differed between the US and the UK.

Finally, we got to the subject of what should we write. And this was the moment I needed to bring out my very best ideas. I had several–some musical, some lyrical–and I opened my laptop to share them.

As I opened iTunes, my co-writer peered over my shoulder and looked at all the songs I'd bought on iTunes. As I scrolled down the many songs by various artists, my co-writer said time after time–

"I've written that title."

and again–

"I've written that title."

After several minutes, I realized that this person had been around the block, had written so many times that they had written a massive number of the titles I had on iTunes. They hadn't written the songs I had on my computer; they were different songs with the same title.

At this point, it dawned on me:

There are many ways to write a title

Titles are not copyright protected. So if you were to run down your iTunes songs, they are all up for grabs. If you can think of a systematic way of developing new ideas around those same titles, then you have an unlimited source of inspiration just by looking down your iTunes catalog. Wonderful.

This whole thing got me thinking. And over the next few weeks, back in my studio in England, I started working with the idea of writing in 3D versus writing in 2D.

What is writing in 2D?

Writing in 2D is what we all do when we start off writing as young songwriters. It's also what you hear too often on the radio, on iTunes and even at church on a Sunday.

A lyric written in 2D paints a picture. It still sounds like a song, often with a lovely melody, cool guitar riffs, sweet harmonies, and a bass line. However, its impact is restricted because it doesn't give us the whole picture. It's flat. It doesn't move us from place A to place B; we just stay in the same place but use different words to describe it in each section.

If I wanted to show you what my house looks like I have a choice. I could draw it in 2D, and it could look like the following:

I know, my drawing skills are so awesome (not). But irrespective of my drawing skills, anyone drawing it in 2D would only provide you with a limited view, leaving questions unanswered: How deep is the house? How far back does the garage go? Is there a patio at the front? Is that a boat at the side of the house or a shed? How thick are the chimneys? Are those front windows really at the sides of the house?

In the same way, writing lyrics in 2D only provides a limited picture because it uses just two dimensions:

- Title (or theme), and
- Structure

Alongside other technical elements (rhyme, rhythm, prosody– matching the tone of the lyric to the tone of the music).

If I were to summarize a 2D lyric, it would broadly look as follows:

Verse 1 - Idea 1
Chorus - Title
Verse 2 - Idea 1, different words
Chorus 2 - Title
Bridge - Idea 1, different words again
Chorus 3 - Title

In short, the ideas presented in each section (other than the Chorus) are identical. They may use different words, but they describe the same thing (the Chorus) in a similar way. There is no "recoloring of the Chorus" to cast a new view on it. There is no movement forward in the lyric. There's no lyrical development. It is a flat picture, without depth of view, without any perspective, and therefore, the emotional impact of any payoff–if it exists at all–is muted (Note: A payoff is where the lyric provides a conclusion or a sense of closure, completion, satisfaction or comfort for the listener).

What is writing in 3D?

Writing in 3D is the work of the lyric pros. It's often something that you only get to do if you have worked with and studied lyrics for a long time (or of course if you've read this book). You may think that I'm overstating the importance of this, but it's a little like looking at a black-and-white TV versus a color TV. Or maybe a Retina display versus a regular display.

Now, drawing my house in 3D would maybe look like the following picture:

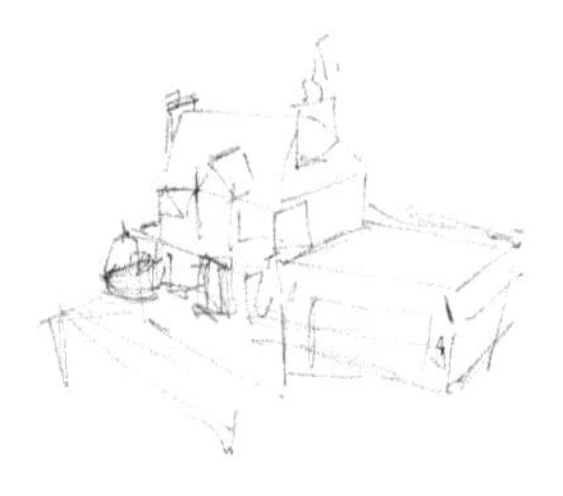

Drawing it in 3D provides a much better representation of my house (believe it or not!). We can see how deep the house is. How far back the garage goes. That there is indeed a terrace at the front. That there's a boat at the side of the house, not a shed. We can see how thick the chimneys are and that there are no windows at the sides of the house.

In the same way, writing lyrics in 3D provides a much more complete picture because it uses all three dimensions of the lyric:

- Title (or theme)
- Structure, **AND**
- **Plot development**

A 3D lyric would work as follows:

Verse 1 - Idea 1
Chorus - Title
Verse 2 - ***Idea 2***
Chorus 2 - Title
Bridge - ***Idea 3***
Chorus 3 - Title

So the ideas presented in each section (other than the Chorus) are DIFFERENT. They move the listener through a journey, they "recolor the Chorus" each time it is heard and cast a new view on it. There is a movement forward that has been crafted into the lyric as it unfolds and develops the plot of the song, starting with Idea 1 and ending with Idea 3. It is a 3D picture with depth, a perspective that is so vivid that the payoff is almost as in your face as it is in the singer's mouth. If that's not too gross.

How Song Maps help

Song Maps help you design your lyric to make sure it is written in 3D by assigning ideas to each section to move and develop your plot as the song progresses. As you'll see later, if you make Song Maps part of your writing workflow you will add 3D sparkle to all of your songs. And you will never want to go back to writing in 2D.

Reason 2 - To save and protect precious creative time

There have been seasons in my life when I've had a lot of time to write and others when I haven't. It's at those times I've often thought to myself:

"Why am I not writing more? Surely there can be nothing more important to me than getting to my piano and writing a song?"

You may have felt the same thing. But part of achieving balance in life is that we can't spend all our time writing. Anything that can help make us more productive during the time we can spend writing is nothing short of a gift. Well, Song Maps are one of those gifts.

Making the most of your creative time

The hours and minutes we spend in the writing room, whether on our own or with a co-writer, are all-precious. Some writers have certain days they can spend writing; some have certain times of certain days.

Whenever you schedule your writing time, Song Maps can help make the most of this precious creative time in a number of ways:

- **It provides a focus for your writing** – By Mapping out where your lyric starts and finishes, you can get a feel for the emotional impact of a song without having to spend three hours writing a complete lyric.

- **It stops you from writing impossible titles** – If you get to the end of the Mapping process, and you are still struggling with what the song is trying to say, you are able to just put it back in your hook book and save it for another day rather than bang your head against a brick wall for hours on end.
- **It stops you from wasting time writing second-rate ideas** – Sometimes titles fall between being able to write themselves and being almost un-writable. These second-rate ideas tend only to show themselves after working on them for a while. By Mapping out your lyric in advance of writing, you can fast-forward effectively to when it's finished and figure out much faster if it is not going to turn out well.
- **It provides a template to write from** – By presenting you with a range of alternative but workable places to go with your idea, you can save time trying to figure out what the next step in the song should be. Especially when confronted with the dreaded Second Verse Curse (more on that later).

In short, by filtering out what can and can't be written upfront, Song Maps will save you a significant amount of precious creative time so with the time you have left you are free to concentrate on the other crafting aspects of writing the very best ideas you have in your Idea Bank.

Reason 3 - To see the full potential of a title

We all have our own ways of writing. Sometimes it's based on what inspires us the most, recent life lessons, conversations we've had or devotions we've read. Sometimes it helps to look at our ideas in different ways. For example:

- Changing the person in the lyric from "me" to "him/her" or vice versa
- Changing the tense of the lyric
- Swapping the second Verse with the first Verse (a helpful trick if you do happen to get stuck on Second Verse Curse)
- Changing the chord progressions
- Changing the key from major to minor or vice versa
- Swapping instruments–e.g., from piano to guitar or maybe even writing without an instrument

All of these things are very helpful for mashing things up to help you write something a little different. But Song Maps take this one step further: it helps you sketch any number of destinations for your title, places that you might not have seen the song going to unless you had a number of predefined lyric routes to apply, and use your imagination to figure out what serves the song best before even writing a word of your lyric.

What happens when you hear a song title?

When you first hear a potential song title, what do you do next? Many commercial songwriters would ask themselves questions like:

- How does that title speak to me?
- Is there anything in real life I could bring to a title like that?
- Have there been any other songs written about that title?
- Is there a similar title that hasn't been written previously?
- What could this song be about?
- Who could I imagine singing this song?

Some songwriters also ask the question,

"Where could this title go?"

This is where Song Maps come into their own–by providing a number of well-trodden development paths. And with these, you can quickly take any title on a journey from where it might start to where it might finish. And then you can play with it to see if a variation might work even better. This is the secret to being able to write ANY song title–including those that you might have thought are impossible to write.

Seeing the full potential of a title

We will look in more detail at how to write with Song Maps in Chapter 4, but the joy of using them is that, within a short space of time (which becomes shorter the more you use them), you can assess five or ten different development paths for any title and from all these possibilities select the option that you consider the most writable, commercial, funny, authentic... whatever result you're looking to achieve.

In short, with Song Maps, you can see a number of options that can be developed from your title with a view to selecting the one that serves your song best. In this respect Song Maps allow you to see the full potential of a title.

Imagine what would happen if you went through your hook book or list of song ideas (wherever you keep them) and briefly applied the seven universal Song Maps listed in Chapter 5 to them? What fresh possibilities could emerge? With the confidence that you can take your title through a tried and tested journey, how much more rewarding will it be to write?

This is one of the biggest benefits I've found of Song Maps: I can look at my titles in multiple ways and select the best one to serve both the song and my co-writer.

Reason 4 - To prepare for co-writes

Co writing has been one of the most wonderful surprises of my songwriting journey. I didn't realize when I first set out how critical it would become, not just to my development as a writer, but to the quality of songs I would write. I also didn't realize how many great friends I'd make along the way.

It wasn't always like this. At the very beginning, the whole idea of sharing my fragile ideas with another human being filled me with utter terror. In fact, when I first heard of co-writing, my immediate reaction was to try to figure out a way of getting out of it.

My first co-write was with someone who had never co-written before either, so we were both newbies, and we went on to write some great songs together. I still love those songs.

In my first ever co-write with a pro, we never actually wrote a word. At the time, he said it was fine. But from where I am today, I realize he was just super kind. Thank you for that, my friend!

I remember once, early on in my co-writing, I was all churned up before a co-write with an amazing writer whom I'd looked up to for years. To make matters worse for my nerves, they'd just won a Dove Award the week before for their part in an incredible song. When they arrived, the first thing I did was congratulate them. And their response was,

"So this is when you find out I'm actually a fraud."

Which was their way of saying they felt almost as nervous and vulnerable writing with me as I was feeling writing with them. And this is typical of the grace, love and humility with which many of my co-writers approach co-writing. Without a doubt, the lessons I've learned about co-writing have been from some of the kindest, most wonderful people I could have hoped to meet in the music industry. Out of the many things they have passed on to me over the years, the one thing that stands out is:

DO WHATEVER YOU CAN TO BEST SERVE YOUR CO-WRITER

It's about doing your best to be your best. But this is probably the subject of another book.

"Next"

While I have been truly blessed with the people I write with, I have heard some horror stories.

One top Country writer told me one such story. She had been set up by her publisher to write with two iconic (male) Country writers on Music Row. It was a three-way co-write and she was the junior writer in the room. This is what we call "writing up."

Once the introductions were over, one of the two veteran writer dudes looked at her and said,

"So what's in your hook book, Darlin'?"

Nervously, she opened her file (she was a paper person) and offered these two demigods her best idea. Before she was able to finish explaining the idea, the other guy said,

"Next."

So she turned the page in her hook book, and the same thing happened all over again.

"Next."

This continued until she finally got to the end of her book, having offered some 40 ideas, which were all met with the same disdain by her co-writers.

At this point, one of the two veterans picked a title out of thin air and started riffing with it on his guitar. Before they knew it, they were writing his idea.

It could be that they wrote the best idea in the room and got a song out of it. But it cost them a relationship because she would never write with them again. The way they went about it–an act of creative terrorism–also trashed my friend's confidence.

My point is this: the way we do things matters. The relationship is greater than the song. But to guard against this happening to us we need to turn up to our co-writes with the very best ideas we can muster; Writable ideas. I'll explain what I mean by a writable idea later in this book.

Building your Idea Bank

Over the years, Song Maps have been invaluable in preparing me for co-writing. They have helped me turn up ready to serve my co-writer as best as I'm able. There is nothing better than arriving at a co-write with a bank of well-thought-out ideas in mind for your co-writer and on hearing the first or second idea they look up from their laptop and with their face lit up they say,

"I'd LOVE to write THAT!"

So, over the last ten years, at any one time I've had around 500 writable ideas in my "Idea Bank." And Song Maps have helped in so many ways:

- At the preparation stage, they enable me to generate a large number of writable ideas quickly to take into a co-write, targeted to the kind of songs my co-writer likes to write.
- In advance of the co-write, knowing that I have done everything I can to provide myself and my co-writer with great ideas during the session significantly reduces the stress of it. Just the act of sitting in a writing room with an amazingly talented writer, frankly, is pressure enough without stressing about coming up with a knockout song idea on the spot.
- During the co-write, by having at my disposal a number of places the song could optimally go, Song Maps allow me to provide options to my co-writer to

help deliver the full emotional impact of the song we are writing.

- Also, during the co-write, if I don't have to worry about where a lyric is going, it allows me to focus totally on other elements of the craft such as structure, rhyme scheme, prosody, words to music, etc.

I have one co-writer friend who often turns up to a session with a song pre-written. She is brilliant, super-creative and super-talented, so it always works. But I'm not sure I trust my own ability to pre-judge what my co-writers will want to write to that extent. I need to have more than one idea up my sleeve.

Also, it's important to some co-writers that they feel they have enough space to contribute to the idea. I had one co-writer early on who, after I had spent a lot of time preparing an idea (to the point that it was over-prepared), rejected it because they said that it sounded like I'd already written it.

So, in my view, having an Idea Bank of writable ideas is better than pre-writing. If you get to the end of this book having completed all the exercises in the Workbook, you will have eight quality, writable ideas in your Idea Bank and twelve Song Maps (7 in this book plus five from the Workbook) for you to walk boldly into a co-write and offer your co-writers, knowing that you will have something tangible to contribute. You may of course decide to write something completely different. But at least you will have done your best to be your best.

Reason 5 - To banish Second Verse Curse

The Second Verse Curse is what sometimes happens after an incredible first hour crafting a killer Chorus, a fabulous supporting first Verse and then... um... you and your co-writer hit a wall.

"Well, where shall we go in the second Verse?" your co-writer asks.

But nothing comes.

You go to the restroom. Nothing's there. You get a coffee and check your writer's mailbox on your way back to the writing room, knowing deep down that when you get back to your co-writer you are likely to experience the most excruciatingly painful two hours of your week while you both bang your heads against a mile-high stone creativity block that no one can dig under, climb over or drive around.

And the brilliance of the first hour of writing seems like a distant memory. Like the creativity fairy is rubbing your nose in what life could have been like if she had continued to stay in the room. Your song goes from a potential #1 hit block-buster to a dud in the space of the five minutes it takes you to realize you've hit the wall.

How Song Maps help

Song Maps get around that. In fact, if you have prepared for your writing session with them, your second Verse will already have been signposted. This is because they don't leave your precious writing session to chance. They allow you, even before you've started your writing session, to fast-forward to the end of the writing process to show you the impact of your song so you can manage the effective placement of ideas.

Alternatively, if you are writing a fresh idea, Song Maps enable you to refer to a range of workable alternatives for where the lyric could go, so you can maximize the emotional impact and, as a result, avoid Second Verse Curse.

As you can imagine, going into a co-write confident that there is no way the dark passenger of Second Verse Curse is going to enter the room is a brilliant feeling and significantly reduces the stress levels, especially when "writing up" with a more experienced songwriter or finally getting to write with one of your bucket list co-writers.

Similarly, if you are writing on your own, it's great to know that Second Verse Curse can never undermine all your hard work crafting Verse 1 and a killer Chorus.

Summary

In this chapter, we've covered five reasons to use Song Maps in your songwriting to transform your lyrics from flat, 2D lyrics into glorious, 3D, full-color lyrics. They will also help you make the most of your precious creative time, enable you to see the full potential of your title by looking at it in different ways, give you confidence in the writing room that you can serve your co-writers well with great writable ideas and completely banish Second Verse Curse from your writing.

The next chapter will take us a lot deeper. I'm going to give you the building blocks of Song Mapping: what exactly Song Maps look like, why we need to honor every idea and explain why the flow of ideas is important in your lyrics. I'll also introduce you to the songwriter's secret weapon (this is awesome) and the fundamental concepts that makeup Song Mapping such as writable ideas and development strategies (Maps). By the end of the chapter, you will be itching to start building your bank of writable ideas for your writing and co-writing sessions.

3 WHAT IS SONG MAPPING?

In Chapter 2, I described why, as a staff writer with Universal Music Publishing, I needed to have access to a bank of writable ideas with me in the writing room when I traveled to Nashville to co-write.

This chapter is crucial. We'll be looking at the building blocks of Song Mapping and what Song Maps look like. You'll discover what to do with ideas when they arrive, the difference between a story and a plot and why the flow of ideas is key to your writing. I'm also going to give you a special gift–the songwriter's secret weapon–before explaining what a writable idea is, the place of Song Maps in generating writable ideas and how they can help you write the best songs of your songwriting career.

Honoring the idea

I'm not sure how to prove what I'm about to say. All I know is that from my experience it's as true as the sun will rise tomorrow morning. It's this:

THE MORE YOU HONOR YOUR SONG IDEAS, THE MORE IDEAS WILL ARRIVE

What I mean by "honor" is, when an idea arrives, whatever you are doing, wherever you are, whoever you're with, capture it and put it somewhere safe.

This can be done in several ways:

- Speak or hum it into your phone
- Jot it down in an email to yourself
- Write it and record it into Evernote (my favorite), or
- Simply write it on the nearest piece of paper you can find.

There have been seasons in my life when my focus has been less on writing and more on other work, traveling, living in a dangerous place (Nigeria, but that's another story). During these seasons, I have found that ideas gradually start to turn up less and less often. It's almost like I've taken off my "songwriter ears" for a time, and until I make a real effort to put them back on again, I'm deaf to the golden song possibilities my subconscious will lead me to in the everyday, ordinary things of life. I have found a similar thing happens with blogging.

For that reason, I'm a firm believer in capturing every idea that comes to me. I keep them in a safe place (ideally in Evernote or Dropbox so they are backed up, and I can access them anywhere at any time). Where you put these little pieces of gold doesn't matter as much as you getting to them at some point in the future.

I have paper napkins, flyers, hotel notepaper going back over 30 years filed in my studio. I will never throw them out. This forms the basis of my Idea Bank of over 500 writable ideas, which are stored electronically in a database, accessible everywhere.

When ideas arrive in your sleep

Have you ever woken up with a song idea running through your head? Sometimes a lyric line, sometimes a melody. There is something special about that alpha/theta state on the edge of sleep that helps imagination thrive. And in that halfway place between being fully conscious and being fast asleep, there have been many blockbuster songs written. At least in my head!

I both love and hate it when this happens. I love it because all ideas are like finding gold, and if they stand the test of fresh eyes and ears in the morning, I have been given a real gift. I hate it because they inevitably mean I have to get out of bed, and either write something down or record something on my iPhone.

I know I'm not the only one who does this.

But sometimes, before I get out of bed, I need to "stress test" the idea in my head to make sure it's worth breaking up my night for. For example:

- **Melody ideas** – I like to hear the whole arrangement moving from, say, the Verse melody to the Chorus, sketch out the highs and lows, the harmonies, the bass, the feel, the groove, the rhythm and the tempo.
- **Lyric ideas** – I like to hear the lyric moving from, say, the Verse lyric to the Chorus, what is each section saying, what rhymes and rhythms could fit with the melody, how does the Pre-Chorus build the idea of the Chorus, how does each Verse recolor the idea in the Chorus, where does the Bridge go before returning to the central theme of the Chorus again. And more.

When we do this with lyrics this is basic Song Mapping: plotting out where the song is going to travel, section by section. We are designing the flow of ideas, sometimes with tried and tested templates i.e. Song Maps, to ensure our lyric has the emotional impact we are seeking to achieve.

Plot versus story

There is a technical difference between plot and story.

A story is only setting out facts. For example:

- The boy was eight years old
- He went to the store
- He bought an apple

Stories set these points out in chronological order and do little to help us understand the context of those facts.

A plot is similar but with one addition: context. For example:

- Gary was only eight years old when he ran off to the store to escape his arguing parents
- It was 2:30 in the afternoon and he still hadn't had any lunch.
- So he bought himself an apple to tide him over.

With this extra context, we can introduce many more colors, emotions and interest. Much of what we are doing with Song Maps is therefore arranging plot ideas rather than simply ordering story facts.

Why is the flow of ideas important?

The movement of ideas is critical to songwriting. Indeed, to any writing. What you already know changes the way you process new information. Therefore, the order in which the listener hears things can dramatically change the emotional impact of a lyric.

Take this example:

The other evening I was on the 15:34 train from London Victoria to Brighton when I saw three preteen brothers behaving very badly. Two of them were shouting and writing their names on the table, and the other was sitting with his feet on the chair, wiping mud off his shoes onto the seat. The carriage was half empty; their Father was slumped in his seat on the other side of the carriage, hiding his eyes, looking like he was trying to get to sleep.

As I watched the situation gradually deteriorate, I was compelled to approach the man and ask him, as politely as I could, to get his children under control. After I had made my request he turned his head, and with bloodshot eyes, he explained,

"Oh, I'm sorry, we are just on the way home from the hospital, their mother passed away this morning, and they are just letting off steam; I'll sort them out."

He sorted them out. And I felt so sorry for even mentioning it.

So in summary, the ideas were:

1. I saw the boys behaving badly
2. I saw the Father was not dealing with it
3. I asked him to deal with it
4. The Father explained the reason
5. I felt sorry for them all

If it were in a different order, I'd still have felt bad for the family, but the impact would somehow have been different. For example:

1. I got talking to the Father, who explained what had just happened
2. I felt sorry for them all
3. I saw the boys behaving badly
4. I saw the Father was not dealing with it
5. But I totally understood

This listing and ordering of ideas are what we do with Song Maps. It is particularly potent for lyric writing because we have the opportunity to paint different sections in different colors (dark and light), which has the impact of maximizing the emotional impact of what we are trying to say.

The songwriter's secret weapon

While I've never been one to go around trying to make people's lives miserable, I discovered a fundamental truth several years ago about what moves people to tears. Or at least, be moved in their own personal way if they are not the tearful type.

This is very much linked to the flow of ideas and Song Maps. It's the songwriter's secret weapon, and I've not seen it written down anywhere else, so you've heard it here first!

I believe it explains why Country songs are all about dogs dying and lovers leaving or running away with best friends. It's the reason there are so many love songs. It's why the gospel story is such a rich source of songs that deeply move people.

People are deeply moved by:

LOVE IN THE FACE OF ADVERSITY

If you think back to all the songs that slew you, that turned you from a happy, carefree person to a blubbering, shaking wreck it will probably be, on some level or another, because you have been confronted with love in the face of adversity.

Look at classic lyrics like the lyric to "I Will Always Love You" by Whitney Houston/Dolly Parton or "Leaving On A Jet Plane" by John Denver.

Maybe the most powerful example I've discovered is a song written by songwriting icon, Phil Coulter, sung by Sinead O'Connor called "Scorn Not His Simplicity." It's not a love song. It's not even a Country song.

When I discovered it, I played it to some friends who'd come for a dinner party, and before Sinead had got to the second

Verse the lady was weeping. When I finally got to talk to Phil, I congratulated him on writing such an incredible song, and even he (with his Irish modesty) admitted that he was very happy with the way it turned out. Without a doubt, it's a powerful song, and it demonstrates, almost flawlessly, the power of this principle to move people. I challenge you to listen to it and not be moved.

So where we place ideas in our lyrics counts. If we place them in a way that shows love in the face of adversity it counts big time. This is also why writing in 3D is so powerful. This is why we will only develop titles to their full potential if we organize ideas into their most powerful order (a writable idea) and then turn them into amazing lyrics that genuinely touch people when they hear the finished song. This is what we do with Song Maps.

What is a writable idea?

A writable idea, as I define it, is the combination of two things:

1. A title
2. A strategy for developing the title (a Song Map)

Writable Idea

So a title on its own is not a writable idea, it's just a title. If I were to go into a co-write with just a bunch of titles, there would be a massive random element as to whether we'd even come out of the session with a song. I believe that to serve my co-writer well, I need to bring more than just a few titles into the room to justify them spending three hours with me, rather than with another writer who may well be better prepared.

Similarly, a Song Map on its own is not a writable idea. It needs to be put together with a title. A title that resonates with both my co-writer and me. The Map on its own is just a way of signposting how ideas flow around that title to recolor it, to expand it, to generate a payoff that somehow justifies the listener spending three to four minutes of their lives giving it some air time. And 99 cents of their hard-earned cash.

What is a title?

One of my favorite books on lyric writing is Successful Lyric Writing by Sheila Davis. In it she says:

"The title is the name of your product, what the listener asks for at the store. Skillful songwriters know how to make a title both unmistakable and unforgettable."

It's a word or phrase that demands and deserves special treatment in terms of where it is placed in the song, how often it's repeated and how it's set up.

I'd suggest a song's title ideally should:

- **Be the "business card" of the song** – the way someone listening to their radio on their way to work knows their way to connect with the song on Apple Music or to buy it from a store.
- **Be the central unifying theme** – or the subject that every section of the song comes back to, recolors and develops as the song moves on.
- **Be logically set up by each Verse + Pre-Chorus** – by ordering the flow of ideas. Often the ideas in Verse 1 may start off some way from the title, but a well-crafted Pre-Chorus can twist the lyric effectively into the Chorus to create a natural progression of ideas into the Chorus.
- **Capture the emotion of the song** – so that a listener can recall the emotional impact of the song simply by hearing the title.
- **Be highlighted by its placement in the Chorus or Refrain** – to spotlight it, the title is often placed in power positions in the Chorus (e.g., first and/or last lines). Also, it is often set up at the end of a Chorus by its rhyme scheme.

I quite often lead open critiquing sessions at seminars where between six and ten brave souls bring their songs to the session (typically 60 minutes long). One by one they play them to me and in front of everyone I listen, make notes and, having got all my thoughts together (it can take a moment or two), I offer advice on what I love about the song and how it could be strengthened (in my view) to make it more commercial.

I call them "brave souls" because I know from experience just how difficult it is to play my newly created songs to complete strangers and to invite criticism from someone who may not understand either where the song has come from or how sensitive I am about it. But full marks to them for having the courage to give it a shot.

What they don't realize often is it's pretty nerve-wracking for me too! These sessions can honestly serve me up anything from a children's musical number about a dying pet to a rock song about how they'd like to throw out their teenage daughter for being rude. The fear I always have is that I would hate to put anyone off their writing because of a throw-away comment I make or a twitch at the wrong time. So these are pretty intense sessions. If the song really has nothing good about it, I would, at least, comment on how nice the font is on the lyric sheet. But sometimes a song can actually make me cry. Both of those are bad moments.

Anyway, in these sessions, I frequently like to keep the title of the song back from the class until it is finished. Then, I ask the class what the title is. Of course, in an ideal world, they should all respond in unison with the right word(s). If not, it's a learning moment for all.

Now that we've got the title under control let's look at the rest of the equation: the development strategy.

Song Maps = the development strategy

A development strategy is another word for the plot, albeit at a high level. Given that we only have a few lines and sections to play with, the more we focus on what an effective plot includes and excludes the more effective our lyric will be. The fact that we sometimes only have a few syllables to convey complex movements in the plot is one of the key challenges for us as lyricists.

I remember watching the film A Perfect Storm. It is one of the few movies I will always remember, but for all the wrong reasons. In theory, it should have been amazing–an incredible cast (George Clooney, Mark Wahlberg), spectacular special effects and a suspense-filled plot based on a true story of a veteran skipper of a fishing boat on a collision course with a massive storm while trawling for swordfish. It has four stars on the iTunes store. It's a Warner Bros. film. James Horner (one of my all-time favorite composers) wrote the score. Everything was going for it.

But when it ended I couldn't have been more disappointed. Basically, after two hours and nine minutes (and that's after waiting for 4.5 GB to download onto my Apple TV), they all died. That was it. Curtains, finito. Of course, it begs the question: "how did they know what happened in the "true story" if they all died?" Very disappointing.

This is what it's like when we have a great title, a hooky melody with some edgy harmonies, a fabulous artist and a great production showcasing the song... but the plot or development of the lyric lets us down. It's a perfect storm in more than one way. Not having the right development can let everything down.

This is why mapping the development of our lyric is so critical if we want to write the best songs of our career. When we map the flow of ideas, we ensure we have all the right things in the right place. We plan for success in our writing. This is where Song Maps come to our aid: a development strategy is represented by a Song Map.

Summary

In this chapter, we've covered why we need to honor every idea, why the flow of ideas is important in writing lyrics, the songwriter's secret weapon and the fundamental concepts that makeup Song Mapping.

The next chapter builds on this to explain how to use Song Mapping. Yes, we are going to get practical! This is important because the process of Song Mapping is just as important as the Song Maps themselves. So I'll introduce you to my four-step process for writing with Song Maps, how to write any title and how to use Song Maps in the writing room.

Exercise

STOP! If you haven't downloaded your copy of the Song Maps Workbook yet, click here:

http://bit.ly/SongMapWorkbook

and download it now! If you have a copy of the *Song Maps Workbook*, this would be a good time to complete Exercise 1 – Collecting Titles.

4 HOW TO USE SONG MAPS

Now it's time to get practical! This chapter is about how to use Song Mapping. This is crucial because the process of writing with Song Maps is as important as the Song Maps themselves. So in this chapter, I will introduce a four-step process for writing with Song Maps, how to write any title and how to use Song Maps to prepare for successful co-writes.

The four-step process for writing with Song Maps

At a seminar once I heard a songwriter hero of mine, Kyle Matthews, speak on the subject of "Where do song ideas come from?" And he said that as soon as he hears a title, he puts it into a framework or structure. He is thinking, "Where can this title go?"

Although he may not know it yet, Kyle is a Song Mapper. Just listen to songs like "You Thought Of Us" (Places) and "The Way We Go About It" (Timezones). We will look at these concepts in detail later. As you make Song Maps part of your workflow, you will soon be Song Mapping in your sleep. Perhaps literally!

When writing with Song Maps I recommend the following four-step process:

1. Select a title
2. Select a Map
3. Draft a writable idea
4. Craft a lyric, refine and rewrite

I normally complete steps 1-3 whether I am taking them to a co-write or not. Step 4 is only when the first three steps generate a finished writable idea that is strong enough to take into a writing session. Unless I'm only playing around, which sometimes is fun in itself.

1. Select a title 2. Select a Map

3. Draft a writable idea

4. Draft a lyric

Step 1 - Select a title

There are a million places to go to find title ideas. They are all around us in conversations, media, and advertising. For me, it's more about being in the right state of mind to hear them. I have picked up some of my best titles in some of the most unlikely places.

Once, I was listening to a stand-in radio presenter (whom I didn't like) for my favorite Saturday morning show who sparked off a title idea that I ended up writing in one of my bucket list co-writes. So I'd recommend keeping an ear open all the time for those little golden gems. You never know when they will appear, and you never know when you might need them.

But if you do need to dig around for titles there are systematic ways of going about it. In Berklee Music School's great course "Writing to a Title," Pat Pattison makes an interesting distinction between:

- **DNA titles** – those that contain their own source of development such as "Black Velvet," "The Tracks Of My Tears," and "Cleaning Out My Closet," and
- **Parasitic titles** – those that take their meaning from the rest of the lyric but by themselves are not that interesting such as "And They Do" or "All I See Is You."

In Sheila Davis' brilliant *Songwriter's Idea Book*, she lists a range of types of titles that we can draw on, such as:

- **Key word titles** – numbers, colors, time (dates, days, months), places, names, top-ten words ("heart," "night," etc.), or book titles.
- **Wordplay titles** – antonyms, idioms, axioms, paragrams (twisting a word of a common expression), coined words (inventing new words), or titles starting with "And..."

Opposites are also helpful in building title possibilities. This is where you combine a negative word/phrase with a positive word/phrase. In the past, I've even used a spreadsheet to generate random combinations until I found one that really resonates (e.g., "Born Crucified"). My friend and fantastic lyricist Gina Boe has a knack for finding these–for example, Mandisa's "Broken Hallelujah" and "Love Like A Thorn." Also, look at the Civil Wars' "Poison and Wine." These are inspiring titles, even before hearing the song and there are many places titles like these can go. And it's wonderful to hear them crafted into such beautiful lyrics.

Other possible sources include:

- Unfinished lyrics
- Key words in other songs
- iTunes
- Films
- Books
- TV shows
- Radio chat shows
- Devotions

- Conversations (yours or other people's!)
- Journaling

Whenever I am considering a title, I tend to think about how writable it is. The aim of Song Mapping is to help us develop one or a few words of a title into a complete story. This is by breaking it down into a set of ideas that move the listener from point A to point B. The more it can be developed, the more writable it is.

If we were to plot titles on a scale of how writable they are, and assume they are evenly distributed across that scale between totally un-writable and totally writable, you should be able to save yourself a lot of time by writing only the top 60% of titles by selecting types 1 through 3, or everything from neutral through DNA titles and "Always going to work" titles.

Spectrum of Writability

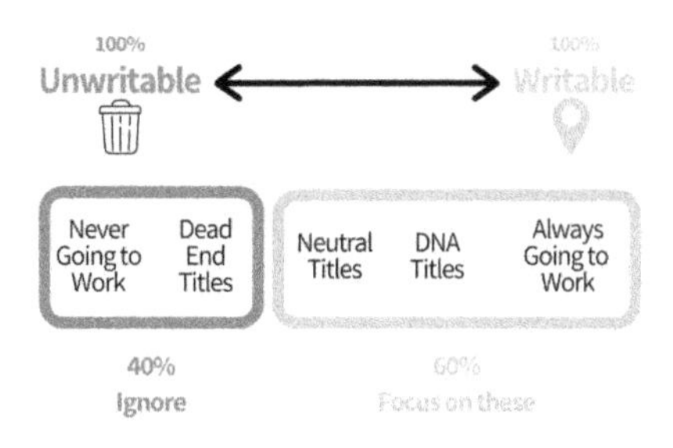

Step 2 - Select a Map

I am going to cover seven universal Song Maps in detail in the next chapter. But your choice of which Map to use is as much a creative decision as your choice of title.

Things you may wish to consider when selecting a Map include:

- The kind of development you can hear most easily working for the title
- The message you want to get across
- The genre of song you are writing
- The artist you are looking to pitch it to
- Where you see the song being sung
- The emotion of the song–is it upbeat, thoughtful, anthemic, etc.
- Whether you can bring anything from your experience to the title
- If it lends itself to a specific story
- If the song might benefit from using different time frames, places or roles
- If you are using word play, plot twist or another device which requires setup
- If there is a variation to the seven Song Maps covered that would work better for your idea

Having looked at the various Song Maps, it is possible that your title will work with some different Song Maps. If this is the case you may wish to think about how the title could be developed for each Map and after that decide which one you will run with.

It's important to remember that this is not a life decision. If you find it's not working out, you can always go back to your second or third choices at a later stage.

Step 3 - Draft a writable idea

Drafting a writable idea is simply the process of assigning elements of a plot to specific sections of your song.

So, having selected your Song Map, this is the time to sketch out how your title will be developed into your writable idea.

As part of this you will have to assume a song form, such as:

- AAA
- AABA
- VCVC
- VCVCBC
- VVCVCBC

Or any other variation you feel appropriate. Note that if your song structure has no Chorus (e.g., AAA, AABA), your Refrain should be used to capture the ideas I have assigned in these Maps from the Chorus.

The way I'd recommend drafting your writeable idea is as follows:

a) Create a structure – Write a heading for each section with the Map Heading next to it. The Song Maps in the next chapter will give you the various headings. For example:

Verse 1 – How the tension is sensed

Chorus 1 – The response

Verse 2 – etc

Make sure to leave room to add a few phrases or sentences (not lyrics) to describe what the section will say.

b) Summarize each section – Underneath each section, use a few words to say what ideas you would like to assign to that section. The key here is to be brief. If specific lyrics come to mind, that's fine–get them down–but writing lyrics is not the focus of this part of the process. It's a kind of mini-brainstorming approach where you try different things, keep what works and archive things you have discarded.

c) Review and revise – Once you have completed this, starting with Verse 1 and ending with the last Chorus, I suggest you go over it again once or twice. Think about the strength and impact of how you have placed the ideas. Ask yourself some key questions like:

- Does it capture the song idea that you originally had (or enhance it)?
- Is there an appropriate payoff?
- Is the Chorus (or Refrain) sufficiently recolored by each Verse?
- Is there anywhere you feel the ideas you have put down do not represent what they are supposed to represent–i.e. does your first Verse really show how the tension is sensed or does it talk about something else?

Remember, it's easier to correct things at this stage than later on.

d) Take a break – When you are happy with it, CONGRATULATIONS! You have your first writable idea in your Idea Bank. And hopefully, it took considerably less time than it would have done to write the complete lyric.

From my experience, it's sometimes very tough to look objectively at ideas until you have had enough space to be able to look at them with fresh eyes. Sometimes that can be 24 hours or longer. Sometimes it's after a nice lunch with a chum.

But it usually helps if you can put some space between drafting this and writing the lyric because during this time it's like you are still drafting in your head, even when you're not. And you may well jot down additional ideas to come back to it with. Nine times out of ten, you are likely to return to your work bringing new perspectives, further ideas and ways to improve it.

e) Final review – Before you take them into a writing session I'd suggest you have a final review of all your writable ideas to try to match them to your co-writer, to make sure they are strong enough, or to see if you can add any further ideas you've had for it.

It's amazing how much more focused I get when I'm looking at ideas just before a co-write rather than at home in the safety of my creative playground.

At this point, you are ready to write a draft lyric. So you might be asking,

"What about the music?"

While there are no rules about how to write a song (just tools, remember?) when writing a lyric-driven song I'd suggest focusing first on the quality of the lyric. This is because (at least in my experience) the music has always been there for a great lyric, even if it takes one or two iterations to get it right. However, if there's a musical riff or motif that you can hear at this stage then it's worth capturing.

Example of a Tension/Response writable idea

Before looking at specific Song Maps in the next chapter, I thought it would be helpful to show you an example of what a writable idea looks like by applying a fairly neutral title, "Follow The Dream", to one of the Maps we will cover in the next chapter, Tension/Response.

Writable idea: "Follow The Dream"

Verse 1 – How the tension is sensed
Weighed by my ordinary life, stuck in a box
Looking out of a dusty window
To where I know I should be
I wanna...

Chorus – The response
Follow the dream, metaphors

Verse 2 – How the solution is sensed
Like the dawn of a new day
A brand new start
Looking forward to the journey ahead
I'll never go back now I'll...

Chorus – The response (*as above*)

Bridge – How I feel about the solution
Grateful to have the chance
Come join the dance, and...

Chorus – The response (*as above*)

To see the draft lyric written from this writable idea, see Chapter 5, Map 1 – Tension/Response.

Step 4 - Draft the lyric

Now that you have your writable idea complete, the process of crafting your lyric follows very naturally.

In each section, you now have a series of keywords and phrases to use as a springboard or focus for writing each line of your lyric.

While these act as a guide for your lyric, it's important how you process new ideas that will inevitably come to you while crafting each line. Clearly some of these will be useful (supporting the function of the section you are working on). These are the lyric lines to keep.

Some of your lyric ideas may take you in a very different direction. It may be that, while these are great, they can't be part of this song right now. I suggest that you capture everything at this point, but whatever lines you don't use simply list them at the bottom of your lyric sheet to keep until you are finished. Or keep for another song next time!

At this stage I'd use a dummy melody to write with, as this will be helpful in forming the rhythm of your lines, the number of syllables you use and highlight opportunities to vary these in a way that develops the prosody of your lyric with the music.

When I do this I hear the music in as much detail as possible– the time signature (e.g., 4/4 or 6/8), the highs and lows of the melody, space for Intros/Outros and if there are any motifs or other things that relate to the production values. Note that the song almost certainly will never sound like the way you hear in your head, even as a demo. But this is all part of building a coherent song and crafting a lyric that matches the music.

In what order should we craft the lyric? My good friend and brilliant songwriter/publisher/author Dave Clark once said:

> "The best way to write a song is back to front."
>
> Dave Clark

And he's right. While there is nothing set in stone, many commercial writers tend to craft the lyric in the following order:

1. Chorus (ideally identical each time)
2. Pre-Chorus 1 (if appropriate)
3. Verse 1 (maybe a double Verse)
4. Pre-Chorus 2 (if not the same as Pre-Chorus 1)
5. Verse 2
6. Bridge
7. Outro

While both the freshly drafted lyric and initial melody are still fresh in your mind, you might want to record a "work tape." This, of course, is not on tape at all but is a rough recorded version on your phone or computer that has the essential elements of the song working together in a format that a publisher (and you!) can hear.

You may wish to hold off sending the song to anyone (except to your co-writer) if you feel you would like to have more time to review or rewrite. As a staff writer, I liked to turn in all of my songs at the end of a writing trip. When I write on my own, I like to spend more time on it, having it on my iPhone (in Evernote), looking at it often and adding to it when fresh ideas come to me.

How to write any title

One of the great benefits of writing with Song Maps is that you can now write pretty much any title by following the above four-step process. And I do mean ANY title.

However, I should make a few points clear:

1. **Not all titles make great lyrics** – while I promise you can write ANY title with Song Maps– i.e. turn any title into a coherent lyric–I can't guarantee they will all be GREAT lyrics. The fact is, some titles are more writable than others and will produce better lyrics than others. And that is why we need Song Maps: to figure out where on the scale of writable/unwritable the title sits before it's too late. After all, you don't want to spend all your precious creative time beating your head against a brick wall.
2. **Working with both sides of the brain** – for

some readers, the approach in this book will seem like I'm suggesting we apply some left-brain, logical processing around what you might consider an exclusively right-brained, creative process. Or putting limitations around something that should be limitless and imaginative. Yes, that is exactly what I'm suggesting. However, I'd ask you to suspend judgment until you have given this a go because I firmly believe you would otherwise be missing a trick. As Phil Hansen says in his brilliant TED talk, "Embrace the Shake," sometimes "Embracing a limitation can drive creativity."

3. **The lyric still has to be written** – Song Maps don't write the songs for you. There's a saying among songwriters that you don't write a song; you rewrite it. This is still very much the case when you use Song Maps. The biggest way they save time is on deciding what you write not so much how you write it. That part of the crafting process is still very individual and down to you to develop in your own way.
4. **Crafting still matters** – when you apply the techniques in this book, it's tempting to think that a mechanical process will work every time. That's certainly not the case. Without a doubt this process will help you write better songs but of course every song needs carefully crafting. So please do bear in mind the other elements needed to create authentic, genuine lyrics that use appropriate language, phrasing, prosody, lyrics to music, consistent rhyme

schemes, etc. because they all matter hugely and will be essential to you in crafting your best songs.

Having said all of the above, in Chapter 5, we will look at how to apply seven universal Song Maps to seven neutral titles and turn them into writable ideas. At the end of this book I will demonstrate how a Song Map can be used to turn even the most impossible title into a writable idea.

Using Song Maps in the writing room

Co-writing is such a great thing–a second pair of ears, another take on where ideas can go, a fresh set of experiences to write from, another set of musical and lyrical influences to draw from, another publisher to pitch the songs...the list goes on. And we each have our respective journeys as songwriters, developing our craft in our own, individual ways.

Some of my co-writers are like you: they devour material about songwriting in books, online, in courses, in seminars and other sources of study. Other co-writers have developed their craft more organically in the writing room, on their own. All of this is fine.

However, whenever a co-write takes place, there will always be some areas of contrast–life experiences, styles of writing, temperament, confidence levels, musical abilities, backgrounds, tastes, and preferences. These contrasts are usually a source of great strength when it comes to crafting a song. When it works out, well, it's almost magical.

However, Pat Pattison, Professor of Songwriting at Berklee Music School, once gave me some great advice:

> "Don't spend valuable time in a co-writing session talking about how to write a song–just write it."
>
> PAT PATTISON

In other words, if you are the kind of songwriter who has developed their craft via books and courses, don't bring the books and courses into your co-write. After all, the writing room is supposed to be a safe place to play, and there is nothing worse than intellectual one-upmanship (or any other kind, really) coming into the writing room. It could be the death of not just your song, but also your relationship with that co-writer.

So while I suggest a process for how you write a song in this book, when it comes to co-writing I strongly suggest leaving the book outside the writing room. However, there are two positives to using Song Maps:

1. **This process is very co-writer friendly** in that it will give you a bank of writable ideas to draw on before you even get into the writing room. Your writable ideas may be taken up exactly as you have drafted them. Or they may not. Your co-writer is likely to have new things to bring to your writable

idea. That is the whole point of co-writing! The point of having a bank of writable ideas is to prepare yourself as best as possible to serve your co-writer. If the co-write ends up taking your idea somewhere completely different (which it may well), then cool, you still have the original idea in your Idea Bank.

2. **The more you use Song Maps, the more intuitive they will become.** After a while, instead of sitting down going through steps 1 through 4, you will begin to hear a title and immediately start Mapping out lyric options in your head. Even in a co-write.

Summary

In this chapter, we've looked at a four-step process to writing a complete lyric using Song Maps, how to write any title and how to use Song Maps to prepare well for a co-write.

The next chapter is the largest chapter in this book where I will give you seven universal Song Maps for you to use with the process described in this chapter right out of the box. They are all fantastic tools to helping you write in 3D, protect your precious creative time, see the full potential of a title, prepare for a co-write and banish Second Verse Curse.

While there are only seven of these Maps, they represent the foundation for developing an infinite set of variations by combining them, mixing and matching new elements and other advanced techniques, which we will look at in our final chapter.

5 SEVEN UNIVERSAL SONG MAPS

In this chapter, I will run through seven universal Song Maps that you can immediately apply to your songwriting. While I'm sure you will discover more, these seven Maps form a foundation for developing many variations by mixing and matching different elements and by introducing new ones.

Every time you listen to a song on the radio or on iTunes, there is an implied flow of ideas embedded in the lyric. I'd like to say every successful song is a great example of well-crafted lyrics but, of course, the reality is not like that.

There are many reasons why songs appear on the radio. However, I'd go as far as to say any really successful lyric-driven song (which generally fall within the genres of Country, Pop, Contemporary Christian Music (CCM), Southern Gospel, Worship, Musicals and Jazz) is more likely to have some strong lyrical development than not. And these can be plotted on a Song Map.

Again, I offer this approach not as rules which have to be followed but as tools which, with a little upfront investment in terms of time, will help you write your very best songs.

The seven universal Song Maps I'll run through here are:

1. Tension/Response
2. Problem/Declaration
3. Timezones
4. Places
5. Roles
6. Twist
7. Literal/Figurative

In each case, I will describe what the Map looks like, how to use it, and give an example of it as a writable idea and a draft lyric before looking at possible variations.

Also, in researching this book, I've trawled through thousands of songs written across all the main genres of lyric-driven songs. I'll therefore include examples of each Map being used in some of the most successful hit songs of all time in these genres.

I would suggest, when listening to the commercial examples, you find a quiet place to listen on your own, close the door put your headphones on and enjoy the ride because there are some spectacular songs referenced here that will both inspire and move you.

The draft lyrics I have written for the purposes of illustrating the Maps here are basic lyrics aimed at illustrating the respective Map, rather than crafting a Grammy winner.

As I said earlier the big difference between using Song Maps and a simple lyric sketch is that, rather than leaving the direction of your lyric to chance, with Song Maps you write using predefined, tried and tested successful templates to develop the title, ensuring effective lyric development and providing you with a solid payoff.

Let's now look at the seven universal Song Maps.

Map 1 - Tension/Response

Tension/Response is the Swiss Army knife of Song Maps because it is by far the simplest and most intuitive to understand. It's also the simplest to apply, being the most common and the most adaptable. When I'm teaching my class I usually say,

"If you go away from this class and try just one Map or strategy, I suggest you make it this one."

It's a great way to start using Song Maps–once you have got to grips with this one, the others are much easier to use because you are familiar with how Maps work.

I love Tension/Response because it is so effective in helping to move a lyric forward. Specifically, it enables us to incorporate contrasts, which are often seen in a lyric in the form of dark and light, low and high, problem and solution (similar to, but not to be confused with, the second Map, Problem/Declaration).

It's particularly helpful to have in your tool kit because it lends itself to virtually any lyrically driven genre–Pop, Country, basically any genre of love song, Christian Contemporary, Southern Gospel, Musicals and Jazz and all songs that seek to move people. Love in the face of adversity.

Another strength is that it helps us use a powerful lyric writing technique: "Show, don't tell." This is because in the first Verse we don't describe what the tension IS, but we are describing how it's SENSED.

For example, consider the difference between:

"I'm going to get on a bus and find myself a better life"

And,

"I'll spread my wings and I'll learn how to fly, I'll do what it takes 'til I touch the sky."

What does Tension/Response look like?

Tension/Response can be represented as follows:

Verse 1 – How the tension is sensed

Chorus – The response

Verse 2 – How the response is sensed

Chorus – The response

Bridge – How I feel about the response

↓

Chorus – The response

How to use Tension/Response

Tension/Response is very straightforward to implement–simply decide on a few things as follows:

1. What is your Chorus (the "response") word or phrase? Does it contain a strong enough idea for the song you want to write?
2. Decide how you would like to build the tension in V1. For example, will it be a feeling, a geographical location, the way someone is looking, a key moment, etc.?
3. Decide what elements of the response you would like to paint in V2; how is this sensed? Again, is it a feeling, an action, a decision, etc.? Be careful not to run into how you feel about the response, which we will leave for the Bridge.
4. How does the singer feel about the response? No surprises here...this will be your Bridge idea.

Example of a Tension/Response writable idea

In Chapter 4 we developed the following writable idea:

Writable idea: "Follow The Dream"

Verse 1 – How the tension is sensed
Weighed down by my ordinary life
Stuck in a box
Looking out of a dusty window
To where I know I should be

I wanna...

Chorus – The response
Follow the dream, metaphors

Verse 2 – How the solution is sensed
Like the dawn of a new day
A brand new start
Looking forward to the journey ahead
I'll never go back now I'll...

Chorus – The response
Follow the dream, metaphors

Bridge – How I feel about the solution
Grateful to have the chance
Come join the dance
And...

Chorus – The response
Follow the dream, metaphors

Example of a Tension/Response lyric

Following on from the above writable idea, here's a draft lyric I wrote, simply filling in the lyric in each section.

Lyric: "Follow The Dream"

Verse 1

For too many days now
Been feeling I'm weighed down
Caged by too many things in my life
I know there is more
'n when I find the door
Nothin's gonna keep me inside
Cause this life is not all it seems
Deep down I know I should really...

Chorus

Follow the dream, follow the dream
Fly where the eagle soars
Sail where the ocean roars
Follow the dream, follow the dream
Running through sun-soaked fields
And follow the dream

Verse 2

Like a blue sky at dawn
Like a baby just born
Now I feel hope fresh like a stream
Each day a new start
Wakes up my heart
Each moment's a step t'ward my dream
Can't wait for the journey ahead
I've come too far to forget, to...

Chorus

Bridge
I'm thankful for the wonder of it all
Don't care if I stumble or fall,
Cause I'll always...

Chorus

A few points I'd make:

1. Note the lyric is written in a 6/8 time signature, which might help you read it.
2. You can see the contrast between the low in Verse 1 ("weighed down") and the high in the Chorus ("follow the dream").
3. You can see how the Chorus is recolored by both Verse 2 and the Bridge, both of which move along the plot rather than simply restating where we were in Verse 1 with different words or pictures.
4. There is a natural lead-up to each Chorus from all three sections (V1, V2 and Bridge). The Pre-Chorus is a brilliant way of making that happen.
5. Notice how there is quite some variation in the

length of line in each section. For example the length of lines in the Pre-Chorus is different from the Verses, the length of lines in the Chorus is different from the Pre-Chorus. As someone who loves writing melodies, I love that variation, especially if a Chorus opens up space for lines to help make good prosody.

6. While the writable idea is incredibly helpful in informing what each section should say, there is some latitude when it comes to actually writing the lyric. For example, the Bridge just worked better using the word "thankful" rather than "gratitude" or "grateful" (and it sings better), and the "stumble and fall" line seemed stronger than "come join the dance" as I'd initially planned.

Variations on Tension/Response

There are many ways Tension/Response can be written. For example,

- It isn't necessarily just about moving from a sad place to a happier place–it can be creating some tension in Verse 1 that is somehow released in the Chorus and developed further in Verse 2.
- Some variations of Tension/Response can be less dramatic and much more subtle–for example, the beautiful crafting of Mark Hall and Bernie Herms in their "Broken Together" by Casting Crowns. There's also a touch of love in the face of adversity

when the Chorus casts a ray of hope: "Could we just be broken together?"

- Some variations are more relative than absolute, e.g., moving from a very dark place to a not-so-dark-but-still-dark place. These can still work really well at the same time as retaining the flavor and authenticity of someone being in a dark place.

Commercial examples of Tension/Response

Examples of Tension/Response are found in every genre and are played every day on the radio. Songs you may want to take a look at include:

Country

"Why" by Rascal Flatts–such a well-crafted song dealing with a very sensitive subject, setting the tension up in V1 ("Must have been in a place so dark"); brilliant metaphor to set up the title in the Chorus ("Why you would leave the stage in the middle of a song?"); V2 the response is "To remember you as you were as a 17-year-old"; Bridge (I think) is "This old world really ain't that bad of a place," with the payoff in the last (modified) Chorus and killer Outro. Lovely song.

Pop

"Breakaway" by Kelly Clarkson–double V1 sensing the tension of living in a small town followed by the song responding in the Chorus with a lovely run-up to the title ("I'll spread my wings [...] to break away"). V2 demonstrating how the response of the Chorus is sensed ("Feel the rush of the ocean") and the Bridge moves the plot forward by telling us how the singer feels about breaking away ("Gotta keep moving on, moving on"). A classic Tension/Response.

"My Shadow" by Jessie J–V1 sets up the tension well ("I wish we could have another minute"), Chorus is the response, a realization ("You're my shadow"), V2 expands on how the response is sensed ("Count to ten and I know you will appear") and the Bridge is how the singer feels about the response ("My heartbeat tapping like it's made of stone"). Another classic Tension/Response.

"Patience" by Take That–V1 tension of love lost, Chorus is "I need time," V2 response is "I wanna start over," Bridge is "I feel scars run deep but I have to believe." Unusually strong lyric crafting for a non-Country British pop song.

CCM

"Broken Together" by Casting Crowns–exceptional crafting of the tension at the start underscored by a spectacular production. Double V1 sets out the tension of how expectations compare with the reality of being together, Chorus responds by offering the solution ("Maybe we were meant to be broken together"), V2 "Sensing, realizing how lonely you must feel," and the Chorus reiterates the imperfect solution, "Broken together."

Southern Gospel

"Never Too Broken To Belong" by Gold City–V1 is a tentative invitation followed by an instruction ("Enter in, make a step"). The Chorus is the response ("When you find Jesus you find your home"), which of course could be heard in two ways ("your home," "you're home"). V2 is how the response is felt ("A peace so sweet, grace that's greater") and the Bridge connects with the listener ("We too were wounded, we know how you feel") to strengthen the invitation that opened the song. Love how it turned out, grateful to my co-writers Michael Puryear and James Tealy for that.

Worship

"Holy Spirit" by Francesca Battistelli–this Grammy-winning song starts V1 with a yearning for being in God's presence ("My heart becomes free," "My shame is undone") followed by the Chorus, which logically moves to an invitation ("Holy Spirit, You are welcome here"). While there is no real V2, which is often the case in this genre, the Bridge continues the prayer ("Let us become more aware of Your presence"), which intensifies the emotion of the whole lyric. I wasn't surprised it got the Grammy as this song stuck out to me from the first moment I heard it.

Other examples of Tension/Response in Worship include "Lord I Need You" by Matt Maher and Hillsong's "Mighty to Save."

Musical

"I See The Light" from Tangled–great tension set up in V1 ("All those days / years watching / outside looking in") followed by the response in the Chorus ("At last I see the light"). V2 is also a new person, a lyric that's reflective of V1 but from a different point of view that still delivers how the solution is sensed. The song ends on a lovely Refrain ("All at once everything is different now that I see you"). Great crafting.

Another example of Tension/Response from a musical is Frank Sinatra's theme from New York, New York, moving from the tension of leaving to go to NY followed by the response of imagining what it's actually like there.

Jazz

"Just One of Those Things" by Ella Fitzgerald (from the musical Lullaby of Broadway)–brilliant crafting by one of the masters, Cole Porter. The tension is set up in V1 with a series of mini-vignettes, all of which match the response about to come but we don't yet know what that response is. That's how he sets the tension. The Chorus simply sums up the response: accepting that it was just one of those things ("Too hot not to cool down"). V2 responds to the Chorus ("So good-bye dear and amen") before sensing it ("here's hoping we meet..."). There's no Bridge but it's still a genius lyric.

Exercise

If you have a copy of the Song Maps Workbook, this would be a good time to complete Exercise #2 – Tension/Response.

Map 2 - Problem/Declaration

Problem/Declaration is similar to Tension/Response, but it moves from an even darker place in the Verses to a lighter place in the Chorus.

Given that the Chorus is saved for a declaration, this has the effect of pushing the "response" from Tension/Response into the Verse 2. As a result, the declaratory nature of the Chorus provides the opportunity to create a much more vivid contrast between the Verses and the Chorus as well as moving the lyric forward by the second Verse being the response.

Problem/Declaration is ideal when we are looking to write a MASSIVE Chorus. Anthemic songs–songs that want to make a bold statement or to capture the spirit of a movement–lend themselves to this format.

The trick with writing Problem/Declaration is that the idea needs to be substantial. For example, there is nothing anthemic about someone losing their shoe (although maybe that's a creative frontier yet to be explored!). The Chorus has to be something people can get behind, something universal enough for people to totally agree with–a cause, an injustice, a purpose or a triumph.

Given the anthemic nature of Problem/Declaration, we see this often in Rock, Pop, CCM, Praise & Worship and modern Hymns.

One thing to note is that anthemic songs can often benefit from simpler Choruses, for example:

Title
Title
Another line
Title

Or simply,

Title
Title
Title

I often think that, as writers of lyric-driven songs, we are sometimes nervous about writing simple Choruses. We feel like we are somehow shortchanging the artist or listener by having a three- or four-line Chorus with a lot of repetition. But if you look at many of the most successful song hits, they often have simple three or four line Choruses with a lot of repetition of the title. Just sayin'.

What does Problem/Declaration look like?

Problem/Declaration can be represented as follows:

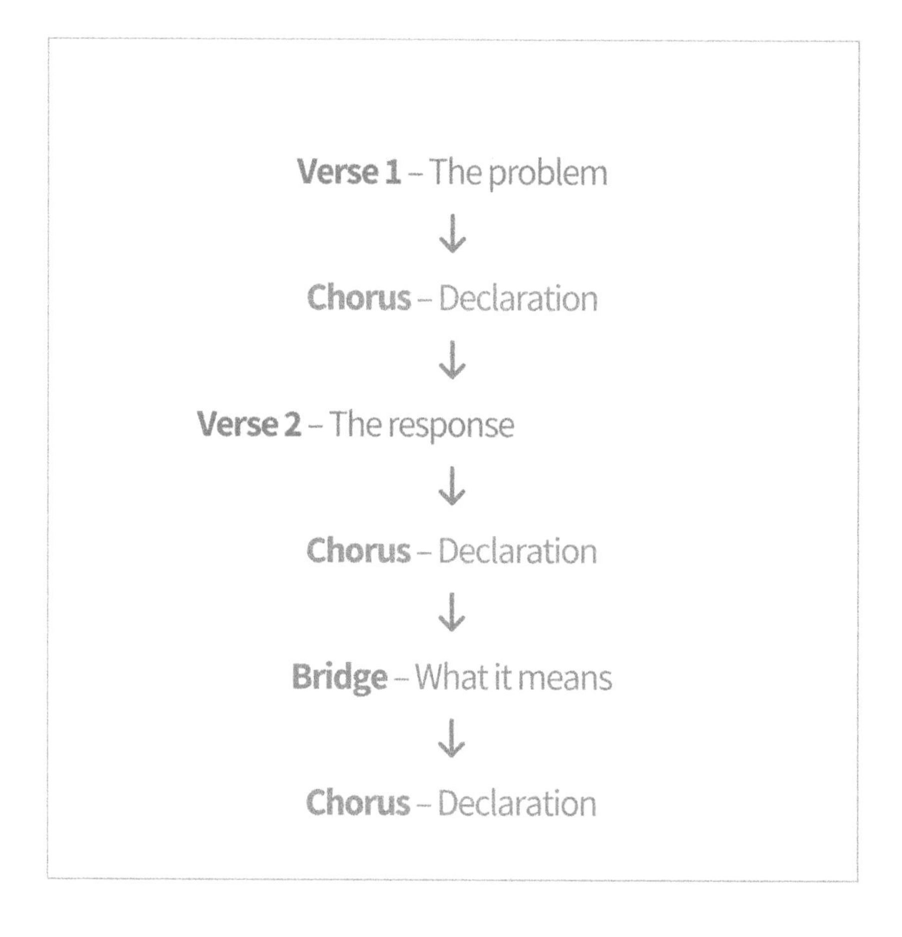

How to use Problem/Declaration

To use Problem/Declaration is similar to using Tension/Response–simply answer a few key questions:

1. What is the "declaration" you want to make in the

Chorus? Is it universal enough, or strong enough to work for the kind of song you are writing? Is it as singable as it needs to be? Repetition is particularly helpful if you are looking to write an anthemic song.

2. What is the problem that prompts the burst of emotion that is declared in the Chorus? This is your V1 idea.
3. What is the natural, authentic response to the emotion behind the declaration in the Chorus? This is your V2 idea.
4. What does this all mean? In other words, having gone through the journey from problem->declaration->response, are there any natural consequences? Has anything changed? In what way will life be different now? This is your Bridge idea.

Example of Problem/Declaration writable idea

Last year, I had the privilege of winning Integrity Music's "Search For A Hymn, 2015". Despite being written as a modern hymn, it was a personal song that I had initially written during a time of extreme uncertainty for a three-billion dollar business I was working with, thrown into turmoil by four out of the five most senior executives being dismissed for taking $50 million in unauthorized payments for themselves.

One night I'd just gotten home from a trip to the Middle East. Feeling exhausted, jet-lagged and beaten up by investors who had lost so much money, in the early hours of the morning I sat in the drawing room of my home and quickly sketched out the following writable idea:

Writable idea: "He Is God"

Verse 1 – The problem
When I feel far from God I'll still trust He's there
When I need someone to fight my battles
When I'm in a storm
I'll rest in the knowledge of His love, 'cause

Chorus – Declaration
He is God, powerful, Creator
Kingdoms rise and fall
But He is God, still

Verse 2 – The response
Man can be selfish, full of pride on this earth
But this is just a small snapshot versus eternity
I'm comforted to know that...

Chorus – Declaration
He is God, powerful, Creator
Kingdoms rise and fall
But He is God, still

Bridge – What it means/eternity
Looking forward to eternity

What an amazing thing to be standing before
His throne
Because...

Chorus – Declaration
He is God, powerful, Creator
Kingdoms rise and fall
But He is God, still

Example of a Problem/Declaration lyric

The writable idea quickly became the draft lyric to "He Is God," which I loaded up to Evernote and polished up over the next few months. Having had the lyric settled for a while I entered it for Integrity Music's "Search For a Hymn" competition last year, which it went on to win.

We tweaked the lyric very slightly in the studio with the help of my fab producer, Trevor Michael, and Chris Lawson-Jones from the A&R team at Integrity, eventually deciding on a double Verse to start with. We also added a musical interlude signaling a change in focus before the last Verse.

Here's the final lyric:

Lyric: "He Is God"

Verse 1
I choose to put my trust in God
No load too much for Him to bear
In each and every battle fought

He is my song and prayer

Verse 2

When clouds and lightning fill the skies
When darkness veils His radiant face
I'll rest in His unfailing love
And His unchanging grace, 'cause

Chorus

He is God, author of all
He is God, of power and awe
Nations rise and nations fall
But He's still God
Yes, He is God

Verse 3

The pride of man and earthly gain
Will only last for one brief hour
So I will put my trust in God
My strong and mighty tower, for

Chorus

Verse 4

One day the trumpet He will sound
To glory He will call me home
And oh what joy that day will bring
To stand before His throne!
I'll stand before His throne!

Chorus X 2

A few points I'd make:

1. This demonstrates how flexible Song Maps can be; although the original Map was a VCVCBC structure, the music I wanted to set the lyric to was much more like a hymn. By having short Verses, a double Verse to begin with and turning the Bridge into Verse 4 it became a slightly different form–VVCVCVCC–which worked well as a modern hymn. There was even space for a musical interlude on the recording before Verse 4 to create a little space as the song reoriented to Eternity.
2. This was an unusual song in that I started with the

melody, which I'd written at least two years previously, just waiting for the right lyric to arrive. This is one of the cool things about writing on your own: you can spend as much time as you like working on a song rather than needing to deliver something to your publisher at the end of a three-hour co-writing session. The reality is, I love writing both ways.

3. The melody already had an anthemic quality about it, starting on a high note and landing nicely on a low note for "nations FALL", all of which helped the emotional impact of the song (prosody).
4. Again, you can see how the Chorus is recolored by the Verses: lows and highs, battles and triumphs, storms and strength.
5. You can hear the final track and lyric video here.

Variations on Problem/Declaration

- **Biblical Truth/Declaration/Response** – which Matt Redman crafts beautifully in "Holy." A point on structure: Worship songs sometimes repeat the first Verse (either with the problem or a buildup of Biblical truths) with a soaring declarative Chorus. If there's no Verse 2, then the Bridge becomes the response, which is a neat alternative in John Mark McMillan's "How He Loves." An unusually wordy worship song but it still works.
- **Problem/Declaration/Prayer** – in the case

of a Worship/CCM Problem/Declaration song, the Chorus can go to a prayer, the Bridge to a reference to Eternity.

- **Perception/Declaration/Reality** – which Taylor Swift so neatly crafts in her song "Shake It Off" on her album 1989.

Commercial examples of Problem/Declaration

Great examples of Problem/Declaration include:

Country

"The Climb" by Miley Cyrus–V1 superbly sets up the problem ("Voice inside saying you'll never make it, my faith is shaking") with the Pre-Chorus leading naturally into the Chorus ("gotta keep trying"). The Chorus resounds with the declaration "There's always gonna be another mountain / that I'll want to move." V2 is all about the solution ("despite it all / no, I'm not breaking") followed by a payoff in the Outro ("Keep the faith, baby"). The Chorus is more hooky than anthemic, but this is an excellent example of how this Map can be used to write a very commercial, highly cuttable song.

Pop

"Shake It Off" by Taylor Swift is another great example of this Map–V1 sets up the problem, which is actually what other people are saying she does (not reality). The Chorus is her declaration that she's just going to shake it off. V2 is her response (reality), which naturally leads back to the Chorus.

The Bridge shows us what it means to shake it off when her ex-man brings his (freaking out!) new girlfriend.

Other Problem/Declaration songs include classic anthems like "I Will Survive" by Gloria Gaynor, "We Are The Champions" by Queen, "Addicted to Love" by Robert Palmer (classic anthemic, simple Chorus but we are made to wait for it - two and a half minutes into the song!), and "Do They Know It's Christmas" by Band Aid.

CCM

"Overcomer" by Mandisa is a superb Problem/Declaration song...and a great song to work out to, partly because of the tempo and partly because of the message! V1 starts with the problem, ("Staring at a stop sign / nothing going right.") The Pre-Chorus introduces God's purpose is greater before the Chorus blasts out the message and title ("You're an overcomer"). V2 turns to sympathize that everyone's been there, and He wants you to know. The Bridge tops it off with the Biblical truth that He wants you to know you're an overcomer. Great work.

"We Are" by Kari Jobe and written by my good friend James Tealy (and co-writers Chuck Butler and Hillary McBride). It's another great example of Problem/Declaration with a darker V1 ("Every secret, every shame") that gradually lifts with Pre-1 to a soaring, killer declaratory Chorus ("We are..."). V2 is a classic response ("We are called, tell the world) before returning to the high of the declaratory Chorus. Lovely writing, James.

Other CCM examples include "Dare You to Move" by Switchfoot Problem set up ("Everyone is looking at you"), Declaration ("Dare you to move"), Response (fallout, resistance, tension), "Forgiveness" by Matthew West (Double 1st Verse, Chorus is a prayer), "How He Loves" by David Crowder (simple, anthemic Chorus, V1 repeated sets the problem, Chorus is the declaration, Bridge is my response).

Southern Gospel

"Over and Over" by Jeff and Sheri Easter and written by two of my wonderful co-writers, Sue C Smith and Belinda Lee Smith, is another great example of Problem/Declaration, with V1 setting up several examples of needing to trust God. The Chorus then declares how God is faithful over and over again (note the nice repetition, which highlights the title and makes it more of a declaration than simply a response). V2 is the real response ("no hesitation that God will do what He says") before some lovely crafting to get us back to the Chorus.

Worship

"Holy" by Matt Redman–a double V1 followed by a simple declarative Chorus, with V2 articulating our response ("our eyes will look on your glorious face"). The Bridge summarizing the meaning of much of the rest of the lyric ("You're all You say You are...").

Other examples include "Cornerstone" and "Oceans" from Hillsong.

Musical

"Thank You For The Music" from the musical Mamma Mia–V1 sets up the problem ("I'm nothing special" except "when I sing"). The Chorus resounds in gratitude "Thank you for the music and giving it to me." V2 is a response to that, asking "How did it all start?" followed by the Bridge asking what it means ("I've been so lucky, what a joy"). I love Amanda Seyfried's version.

Jazz

"Nothing's Gonna Change My Love For You" by George Benson–V1 really sets up the problem nicely ("If I had to live my life without you") before the Pre-Chorus turns that around ("I don't want to live without you") and the declaratory Chorus ("Nothing's..."). V2 is the response to the Chorus ("If the road is not so easy") with a nice simile thrown in ("like a guiding star"). Nice work by writers Gerry Goffin and Michael Masser, penning an Adult Contemporary song turned into jazz by Benson.

Exercise

If you have a copy of the Song Maps Workbook, this would be a good time to complete Exercise #3 – Problem/Declaration.

Map 3 - Timezones

This is a great Map for telling stories. The story starts in Timezone 1 leading into the Chorus, which sums up a theme with the title. This moves to a new situation in Timezone 2, which recolors the theme of the Chorus (the title) before moving to Timezone 3 or delivering the payoff either in the Bridge or a third Verse (if required).

Throughout this Map, the Chorus remains the binding or common element that unifies the song. The Bridge can also be used to resolve the story.

Timezones is (pardon the pun) a timeless development strategy, having worked as well in the 1950s ("Anything Goes," Ella Fitzgerald) as it does in 2016 ("7 Years," Lukas Graham, which is #1 in the UK pop charts as I type). You can even see an element of Timezones being used in John Newton's "Amazing Grace," which was published in 1779.

Given that this Map lends itself to telling stories, Timezones is perfect for Country songs, Pop, CCM, Southern Gospel and Worship. It's a brilliant opportunity to demonstrate the craft of lyric writing in that the Chorus (the title) ideally should be identical but also work for every Timezone. When this is done well it nearly always creates a "wow" moment that is not just impressive but is often moving and makes for a highly memorable song.

Whether Timezone 3 is in a Bridge or a third Verse is a creative judgment about the length of the song. If the Verses are already quite long, then it may be better to have Timezone 3 in a Bridge, which can be (and maybe should be for the sake of contrast) a lot shorter in terms of number of lines. Or maybe not even have a Timezone 3 at all.

One word about tenses: it's very easy to get totally messed up on tenses when writing a Timezones song. If you're not careful, you can end up spending half of your precious words trying to tell people what year it is! So one way out, which I used in the song below, is to have the whole song in the present tense but signpost the Timezone in a narrative way. It simplifies everything.

What does Timezones look like?

Timezones is great at presenting two or three time-bound scenes or scenarios to demonstrate whatever the message is in the Chorus. It automatically enables you to move the story on because, well, the Timezones do it for you. Two things you need to think carefully about:

1. Ensuring the Chorus works equally well after each Timezone.
2. Making sure there is an appropriate payoff in the Bridge/Verse 3.

Timezones can be represented as follows:

How to use Timezones

To use Timezones it might be useful to ask yourself the following questions:

1. What is the central theme or idea you want the title to represent? What idea is universal enough to be

approached from two or three different Timezones? That becomes the idea for your Chorus.

2. When does the story start? How can you articulate that? What senses can you draw on? Who is involved? What are they like? This is V1.
3. When does the story move on? How can you paint that picture lyrically? What senses can you draw on this time? How does it differ from V1? This is V2.
4. What does this all mean? Are there any natural consequences? How can the story resolve? How can it mean more to the listener? What lessons can be drawn from this story? These are the ideas to use in your Bridge.

Example of a Timezones writable idea

Here we will look at a song I wrote called "When You Lose Your Dad." It's a perfect type of title for Timezones because you can go back into childhood memories and move forward to other key moments in the future. One of the difficulties I had was trying to find a suitable payoff because, how can there be any payoff from such a dark moment? But there was, and I love how it developed, albeit in the very last moments of the song.

Writable idea: "When You Lose Your Dad"

Verse 1 – Timezone 1

Going shopping with my dad and suddenly getting lost

Feelings of shock, world turned upside down,
lost without him

Chorus – Title
There's nothing worse than losing your dad

Verse 2 – Timezone 2
Funeral scene after losing him suddenly
Thought he was healthy
Same feelings of shock, world turned upside
down, etc.

Chorus – Title
There's nothing worse than losing your dad

Bridge – Payoff (signaling)
Metaphor, how it doesn't seem right he's gone

Chorus – Title
There's nothing worse than losing your dad

Verse 3 – Timezone 3
Now, noticing something familiar
How I talk to my kids,

In many ways, because of your DNA, you never lose your dad

Example of a Timezones lyric

So, turning to the lyric again, this was another personal song for me given that this speaks right into my experience of losing my Father. I had a melody first, which I was keen to set the lyric to–a 6/8 mid-tempo Country-sounding song. I wrote the lyric over a number of months before showcasing it and tweaking slightly afterward. When I performed this in a concert alongside a group of Nashville songwriters, one of my great friends came up to me and said to me,

"You had us hanging there until the very end!"

Anyone who's lost their Father would understand that I needed to have that resolution just to keep myself together long enough to sing this live.

Lyric: "When You Lose Your Dad"

Verse 1
As a boy only four
At a Saturday mall
I'm hand in hand with my dad
In the store where we are
With toy soldiers and cars
I'm lost in my own wonderland
One minute he's here beside me
The next my world's turned upside down

Chorus

With him gone
I suddenly feel so alone
With him gone
Who's gonna take me back home?
No one should say that they know how
you feel
When you feel like you'll always be sad
When you lose your dad

Verse 2
Many years on
I'm at church with my Mom
Trying to hold back the tears in my head
We knew he was eighty
But thought he was healthy
Now he's healthy in heaven instead
One minute he's here beside me
The next my world's turned upside down

Chorus

Bridge
Like the sky on a moonless night
A reflection of heaven is gone
And it doesn't feel right

Verse 3
Here in the mirror
I'm trying to figure out

Something familiar in me
In the way that I look and I speak
Now I'm older it's easy to see

Outro
You never lose your dad
You never lose your dad
When you lose your dad

Some points I'd make:

1. I wrestled for some time whether to put the payoff ("You never lose your dad") in the Bridge, in a last Verse or an Outro. The decider was when I realized the payoff needed to be built up, which meant that V3 had to come before the payoff. Plus, I was very happy with the way the Bridge came out–as a Father of three, I am only too aware of my responsibility to be a role model to them–the reflection of heaven is part of who my Father was to me.
2. See what I mean about keeping the lyric in the

present tense and signposting the Timezone in the narrative? "Boy only four"–"many years on"–"here in the mirror." It seemed to work fine and got around any potential tense issues.

3. The structure is also not quite standard–VCVCBVO–with the Outro being an important part of the song. This again demonstrates that you can be flexible in where you place the ideas in your song; just make sure you get there by the end.

Variations on Timezones

Just like with the other Song Maps, there are many ways Timezones can be written. For example:

- Timezones can move many years during a song (see the fabulous crafting by Kern and Hammerstein in Ella Fitzgerald's "Anything Goes") to several years (Steven Curtis Chapman's "Cinderella") or even just a few minutes. The important thing is to support the central theme in the Chorus with each scene or Timezone.
- One cool technique to unify the song in the Chorus is to relate to both Timezones. For example in Jana Kramer's wonderful "I Got The Boy" the Chorus starts, "I got the first kiss and she'll get the last," which sets up the Chorus wonderfully to land on "I got the boy, she got the man."
- Another cool technique is to use the lessons from

the past to signal a better outcome in the future, to create a compelling payoff for the lyric. In Kelly Clarkson's emotional "Piece by Piece," she reflects on her own Father's shortcomings in bringing up his daughter. The last Verse starts, "Piece by piece I fell far from the tree / I will never leave her like you left me." Wonderful crafting.

- In Miley Cyrus' "Butterfly Fly Away" the combination of Timezones with a great metaphor works so well in painting pictures of her growing up. The recorded track totally nailed this by her Father singing on the track too.
- A popular use of Timezones is in modern hymn writing when, in the last Verse or Bridge, a song reflects on Eternity to establish a payoff, something I did in my modern hymn "He Is God" as did Matt Redman in "10,000 Reasons."

Commercial examples of Timezones

Examples of well-known Timezones songs include:

Country

"Without You" by Keith Urban–V1 is right at the start when they first looked/smiled at each other ("the very first day"). The Chorus neatly sums up the idea of the song–despite all the traveling; it would mean nothing without her ("Good as gone without you"). V2 fast-forwards to when they have a baby girl and paints a lovely picture of an extended family

("People that I barely knew / They love me 'cause I'm part of you"). The Bridge takes the idea of the song one step further, stating that without her he'd just be going through the motions of life. Perfect.

Other great examples of Timezones include "Three Wooden Crosses" by Randy Travis, "I Got The Boy" by Jana Kramer, and "Butterfly Fly Away" by Miley and Billy Ray Cyrus.

Pop

"7 Years" by Lukas Graham–an almost unique life story starting at seven years old and proceeding to eleven years old, twenty years old, thirty then sixty years old before returning to seven again. "Piece by Piece" by Kelly Clarkson is another powerful song spoken to her Father in a brave, moving and what seems a very personal message to him with a very effective use of Timezones.

CCM

"Cinderella"by Steven Curtis Chapman–a moving tribute to his daughter who sadly passed away but starts with her as a child, growing up and going to the prom, getting married to her husband; some lovely crafting. Another great Timezones song is "Time In Between" by Francesca Battistelli, moving elegantly from the beginning of time, the time of Jesus' birth, to the here and now.

Southern Gospel

"Lazarus Come Forth" by Carman is a classic "inspo" song that tells the story of Lazarus in a very dramatic way, demonstrating the storytelling power of Timezones with added color and humor that Carman brings to it.

Worship

While storytelling is not used as a device that much in Worship, as discussed above, there are instances when Timezones can be usefully employed–"10,000 Reasons" by Matt Redman, "Amazing Grace" by John Newton, "He Is God" by Simon Hawkins.

Musical

"Hello Young Lovers" from The King and I–Richard Rogers and Oscar Hammerstein's richly crafted song where the singer sings to the lovers, reflecting on her experience of being a young lover.

Jazz

"Anything Goes" by Ella Fitzgerald– expertly uses Timezones to craft a song in AABA format with the Refrain effectively taking the place of the Chorus in the Map. V1 reflects on "olden days" (Timezone 1), the B section and V2 is in today's time (Timezone 2). "Miss Otis Regrets" by Ella Fitzgerald is another lovely, classic Timezones song, only taking just minutes to move from one Timezone to the next rather than years between each Verse.

Check them out–it's incredible how relevant and timeless this approach is. If you haven't got a Timezones song in your catalog already, I'd encourage you to have a crack at it.

Exercise

If you have a copy of the Song Maps Workbook, this would be a good time to complete Exercise #4–Timezones.

Map 4 - Places

This is also a great Map for telling stories, with the plot unfolding in different locations rather than at different times.

This Map doesn't necessarily require you to use the name of different countries or cities; it just needs to give enough information about the different places for the singer to establish the plot development. It could even refer to various states of mind or "places" the singer might be in.

Much like with Timezones, the fact that different places are used in each Verse (and maybe the Bridge as well) means the story is more likely to move forward naturally. This also means the Chorus, as the unifying element of the song, will need to work well for every place the song goes.

One tip: to make a Chorus work well with different Verses in this Map, a neat trick is to zoom out from the specifics of your lyric to summarize the heart of your lyric in the Chorus. This way you are not committed to figuring out how to work in the same set of fine detail in each Verse. One way of doing this is to build a simpler Chorus, maybe repeating the title two or three times with an offsetting line with a setup rhyme for the last line, which may well contain the title.

Places is another great Map to use for storytelling, so this is perfect for writing Country, Pop, Southern Gospel and other genres.

Of course, there's an opportunity to get poetic with the lyric in developing subplots, so the song moves literally from one place to another but also moves the characters from one place to another metaphorically.

What does Places look like?

With Places, we paint a picture in Verse 1, which sets up the idea of the title in the Chorus.

Verse 2 moves the story along, but from a different place, before again setting up the idea of the title in the Chorus. The Bridge can either be a third place and/or the payoff of the song.

The trick to this Map is to ensure an effective return to the Chorus from the different scenes or scenarios painted in the Verses and the Bridge, maybe using a Pre-Chorus set up.

While the most obvious use of this is to reference different geographical places, it is totally applicable to any "place" whether geographical, emotional, stress level or other dimension that you would like to write from. Or maybe even combine them?

The Places Map can be represented as follows:

Verse 1 – Place 1 – the story begins

↓

Chorus – Title

↓

Verse 2 – Place 2 – the story moves on

↓

Chorus – Title

↓

Bridge – Place 3/Payoff

↓

Chorus – Title

How to use Places

In working with Places it might be helpful to answer the following questions:

1. What is the central theme or idea you want the title to represent? Could this work with two or three different places? How would the dynamic of

different places impact this central theme or idea? When you find this, it will become your Chorus idea.

2. Where does the story start? What does that place look like? What senses can you draw on? Who is there? What are they like? This is V1.
3. Where does the story move on to? What does it look like? What senses can you draw on this to show what this new place is like? How does it differ from V1? This is V2.
4. What does this all mean? What is the payoff? Can the story resolve? How can it relate to the listener in today's time? What lessons can be drawn from this story? These are ideas you can use in your Bridge.

Example of a Places writable idea

You could argue that there are elements of this Places Map in "When You Lose Your Dad": in a mall, at a church and "in the mirror." But here's another writable idea, this time about a childhood sweetheart, just to illustrate it further.

Writable idea: "How Many Times"

Verse 1 – Place 1

Driving past the little school where we met
Memories flood back, I miss you
Please tell me...

Chorus – Title

How many times do I need to say goodbye
When I think of you I realize
I'll never be the same

Verse 2 – Place 2
Walking past our favorite restaurant
Remember the good times
I wonder...

Chorus – Title
How many times do I need to say goodbye
When I think of you I realize
I'll never be the same

Bridge – Payoff/Place 3
Landing at Dulles, coming home from NYC
I never want to be away from you again

Chorus – Title
How many times do I need to say goodbye
When I think of you I realize
I'll never be the same

As a writable idea it is only a simple sketch of a song, with no rhyme or proper lyric lines. The focus in drafting the writable idea is to get the idea flow for the plot right before going on to draft the lyric, which I will do here.

Example of a Places lyric

So, developing the above writable idea into a lyric, here's a draft that simply fills in the lyric for each section.

Lyric: How Many Times

Verse 1
I'm driving past the school where we first met
Windows filled with paper art, yellows, blues and reds
The corner of the playground
Where we stole our very first kiss
There's a brand new classroom, toys and deck
But, I'm thinking coming here was a mistake
I can almost see my childhood sweetheart's face

Chorus
How many times do I need to say goodbye
How many times do I need to feel the pain
A thousand miles from me
But everywhere I see you
How many times do I need to say goodbye

Verse 2
I'm walking past our favorite restaurant
Where we used to go each Valentines Day, stay there till it's late
We'd start out drinking rosé

And finish with two reds
Then we had our kids and couldn't stay
the pace
Oh coming here again what can I do?
I'm aching to be home again with you

Chorus

Bridge
Now landing here at Dulles
Coming home from NYC
Tho you never usually come here
I really hope you're meeting me
When you see me in arrivals
The girls come running in
How could I ever leave you here again, yeah

Chorus

Some points I'd make:

1. Assigning one location to each Verse helps provide space to introduce "furniture"–not real furniture, but

pictures of real objects to help paint pictures of what's happening in our lyric plot.

2. When we get to the Chorus, we've already mentioned the childhood sweetheart, although we are not totally sure if this is the "you" in V1, although it probably is.
3. V2 moves the song on not just in terms of place but also in time–going to restaurants, wine, staying up late, children coming along. The same pain of the Pre-Chorus, remembering the singer's childhood sweetheart, is common to both V1 and V2.
4. The setup to the second Chorus tells us that the spouse is at home.
5. The Bridge takes us to yet another place, Dulles Airport, where the family is reunited and the song resolves, the mystery is over, and we have a double meaning for the title "How Many Times": multiple people (a wife and two daughters to say goodbye to) and multiple trips this guy reluctantly takes on business.

Variations on Places

You can create new variations of this Map in a number of ways. For example, you could use different specific geographical locations in each Verse to create movement. Or you could pan out from a specific place to somewhere more general, such as moving from a room in Verse 1 to a town/city in Verse 2. Or you could go from a specific place in Verse 1 to a general global perspective in Verse 2.

It is also possible to apply Places in a slightly difference sense–such as moving to different emotional places, spiritual places and use this as a way to develop your lyric–e.g., from sad to happy, from broken hearted to falling in love, from a place of loneliness to a place of feeling loved or from a place of doubt to a place of faith. The only limit on how far we take Places is the limit we put on our own imagination.

Commercial examples of Places

There are some great examples of using Places across all genres. Examples I'd highlight include:

Country

"My Town" by Montgomery Gentry–lots of "furniture" in all three Verses and a lot of detail and color in the Chorus underlining the central theme of the ups and downs of living in a community. Also an element of Timezones, with subplots around the water tower and tractor. V3 is where we get a lovely set of payoffs with the rusty tractor in V1 now painted up and in the front yard, and Jenny, whose name was painted on the water tower in V1, now with a kid and going to church with the singer.

Another great modern Country example of Places is "Fly Over States" by Jason Aldean.

Pop

"Love Story" by Taylor Swift–some really nice storytelling and plot development here: the geographical position isn't a different country or city, but different geographical places in the same residence or town. The lyric moves from the balcony in V1 to the garden in V2 and then to the outskirts of town in the Bridge, ensuring that the story develops along with the movement of the characters in the lyric. By the end of the song both characters are ready to run away with each other because they have moved both physically and emotionally. Very nice crafting.

Incidentally, it's great to see such lyrical crafting in a Pop song. I'm thinking Taylor's Country, lyric-driven roots helped her with this as a crossover artist.

Other classic pop lyrics you may like to look at include "Amarillo" by Tony Christie (which, despite its comedic association with Peter Kay, is actually well written), "Walking in Memphis" by Marc Cohn/Cher, "Never Forget" " by Take That, which uses Places in a more metaphorical sense–in V1 the singer is yearning for stardom, in the Chorus the singer is valuing where they came from, in V2 the singer appreciates the journey.

CCM

"You Thought Of Us" by Kyle Matthews is a brilliantly crafted Places/Timezone song, which tracks the Easter story in a series of vignettes from Judas' betrayal, the crucifixion, and the resurrection all told in a brilliantly lyrical way.

Southern Gospel

"Sometimes It Takes A Mountain" by the Gaither Vocal Band– moves through different places of a metaphor, from facing a mountain in V1 to a place of surrender in V2 and the acknowledgment in each Chorus that sometimes that's what it takes to "get a hold of me." Good job.

Worship

"Indescribable" by Chris Tomlin–snapshots of inspirational physical locations to illustrate the title ("highest of heights to the depths of the sea," etc.).

Musical

"My Girl Back Home" from South Pacific–an excellent example of Places and the kind of high-quality lyric crafting we often see in musicals. While this doesn't follow the Map, strictly it visits everywhere from Princeton to Southeast Asia.

Jazz

"You're the Top" by Ella Fitzgerald–a Cole Porter special and an extraordinary mix of places/roles/food/other objects! But it shows that Places can be an effective way of developing a lyric, especially with the title set so perfectly ("If I'm the bottom, you're the top").

Exercise

If you have a copy of the Song Maps Workbook this would be a good time to complete Exercise #5–Places.

Map 5 - Roles

Roles is another lovely Map for developing a plot or story.

Roles could mean any number of things, the obvious being different characters. It could also take on different viewpoints, such as my feelings for you and your feelings for me (e.g., "Thinking Out Loud" by Ed Sheeran) or what I think of you and what you think of me ("Blank Space" by Taylor Swift).

Again, there are great examples of the effective use of Roles across all genres of music, in Country, Modern Country, CCM, Pop, and in Musicals and Jazz.

What does Roles look like?

Roles is a great technique to build the context of a title by spotlighting different points of view on the same idea. It is similar to Timezones and Places insofar as we are using different scenes to drive the song forward.

It's also very effective because with each section we can include a lot of "furniture," or specific detail, to recolor the Chorus from fresh perspectives.

The trick with Roles is not so much what characters or perspectives we spotlight, but the very best crafting will move the story on with each section rather than just repeating essentially the same message two or three times. So we are looking for plot development at the same time as fresh perspectives.

Roles can be represented as follows:

Verse 1 – Role 1

↓

Chorus – Title

↓

Verse 2 – Role 2

↓

Chorus – Title

↓

Bridge – Role 3/Payoff

↓

Chorus – Title

How to use Roles

In working with Roles, the key decisions you will need to make are as follows:

1. What is the main idea for your lyric? What word or phrase sums it up? From this, you can decide on your title and therefore the idea that you will assign to the Chorus.

2. In what role will your lyric start? What are they thinking, feeling, looking like? Are they happy, sad, emotional? Are they going somewhere? Show the listener what this person looks like. How does this person relate to your Chorus? This is your V1.
3. In what role will your lyric move to AFTER the big reveal of the title in the Chorus? Are they happier, sadder, more emotional? Have they arrived somewhere? Again, show the listener what this person looks like. How does this person return and relate to the Chorus again? This is your V2.
4. What is the payoff or conclusion? How does this relate to the character(s) highlighted in V1 and V2? What does this link mean? Then, how does this lead back into the Chorus? This is your Bridge.

Example of a Roles writable idea

Writable idea: "Time"

Verse 1 – Role 1

Teenage girl wakes up upset that her boyfriend wants to break up, she cries in her mother's arms, who says -

Chorus – Title

Just give it time
Time is a healer

Verse 2 – Role 2

Her boyfriend thinks he loves her but he's too young to commit, praying he hears a voice saying...

Chorus

Just give it time
Time is a healer

Bridge – Payoff

Give yourself time to get over it and to find 'the one'

Chorus

Just give it time
Time is a healer

Example of a Roles lyric

Based on the writeable idea above, here's how the lyric could look for "Time."

Lyric: "Time"

Verse 1

Seventeen and she wakes up so sad
The text on her phone proves the doubts she had
It's from this boy and her tears fall like rain
It's like her life's over, never be the same
Growing up so fast but still young

Crying hard in the arms of her Mom
And tenderly, wiping her tears
Her mother weeps with her
And then she whispers...

Chorus
Just give it time (time, time)
Just give it space (space, space)
If you wanna feel better
And find the smile on your face
Give it time (time, time)
And you will see
After a while
That time is all you need

Verse 2
At twenty-one he is too young
To know how he feels about anyone
A lifetime ahead and decisions to make
One life to live, just one heart to break
Tho' he said he'd fallen in love with this girl
It's too much and to soon to change his world
So silently, down on his knees
He starts to pray and
Hears a voice saying

Chorus

Bridge
Time to get over it, time to look back

Time to feel happy with the place that you're at
Time to grow closer to someone who cares
Someone who loves you with no doubt or
regrets, so

Chorus

Some points I'd make:

1. It's easier to write a Chorus that works with each character if the characters are somehow linked – e.g., girlfriend and boyfriend in the case of "Time". In Montgomery Gentry's "Something To Be Proud Of", it's a Father and son.
2. Although it's tricky to demonstrate this without hearing the tune, the timing in the Chorus melody mirrors the time and space in the lyric (time, time... space, space).
3. The Bridge provides the payoff – building on the idea that 'time is a healer', it goes one step further to say time is the opportunity to find someone who loves without regrets or doubts. Too subtle to call it a twist but it's going in that direction.

Variations on roles

While it is logical to assign a different role to each Verse, recoloring the title as the song progresses, there are some alternatives to this.

For example,

- Two roles woven into each section in either a conversational duet or expressing the same thing from two different points of view (e.g., "Summer Nights" from the musical Grease)
- Assigning V1 and V2 to two different people with the Chorus assigned to a third but common person (e.g., V1 a son, Chorus the Father, V2 a daughter, or V1 poor man, Chorus God, V2 rich man)
- To mash up Roles with Timezones and have the same person address the same title but from different ages or times in their life
- Assign V1 to a person, V2 to the group the person is part of (e.g., Beth Nielsen Chapman's brilliant "Child Again")

Commercial examples of Roles

Great commercial examples of Roles across the various lyric-driven genres of songwriting include:

Country

Montgomery Gentry are masters of crafting hit songs with Roles. "Something To Be Proud Of" is a great example of this at the same time as touching a great universal emotion–having purpose and pride in what you do with your life. V1 is role 1–the singer's Father who tells stories about flying F-15's in the war–before the Chorus which sums up what it means ("that's something to be proud of") with some lovely examples of what it looks like ("chins held high as the tears fall down") before setting up the rhyme agent for the title ("in the arms of the woman that you love"). Great crafting so far. V2 is role 2–the singer himself not having the journey he felt his parents wanted for him, again with some lovely furniture ("Sure do miss that old hot rod") before asking his Father if he is ashamed how he turned out. A great setup for a new Chorus ("Said, 'let me tell you right now'"), which works well. The Bridge is a wonderful summary of the song ("if all you ever really do is the best you can, you did it, man"). Brilliant.

Other examples or Country Roles include "Hell Yeah" and "Roll With Me" by Montgomery Gentry and "Mountains" by Lonestar (a favorite of mine).

Pop

"Blank Space" by Taylor Swift is a great example of how to apply Roles in a modern pop setting. A double V1 is written in conversational language from role 1's perspective of "what I think of you" ("My next mistake") before a double Chorus, which takes a step back to describe what's going on ("I love the players and you love the game") and a sinister title setup line ("I've got a blank space, baby, and I'll write your name"). A double V2 summarizes her words from role 2's perspective, which is "what her target will think of her" as the relationship matures (from "cherry lips" to "screaming and crying"). The Bridge is the payoff, ("boys only want love if it's torture"). Excellent writing from Taylor.

Another example of Pop Roles is "We Will Rock You" by Queen, in which three Verses address three different generations (boy, young man, old man).

CCM

"I Need A Miracle" by Third Day does a great job spotlighting two different desperate people in V1 and V2, with the Chorus summing up the good news. Then in V3 the payoff comes ("And on that night, they found a miracle") which links up the two desperate situations with the solution. Very nice writing.

Also,"Freedom Song" by Mandisa spotlights four people in similarly difficult situations: a child from a broken home, a man with addictions, a sixteen-year-old with no self-esteem and a wife who's lost and trading dreams for a busy life. The Chorus each time declares the timeless scriptural truth that resolves each situation ("I have been set free").

Matthew West's "Life Inside You" is another example of a well-crafted Roles song with a lovely twist at the end. Check it out.

Southern Gospel

"The Body and Blood" by Janet Paschal is a spectacular example of how to execute the Roles Map in a Southern Gospel format. V1 tells the story of character 1: a lady who gave her only child away for a life ("Easy to regret".) The Chorus then moves to the sacrament and a very personal address from the Savior himself. V2 then goes to character 2: a troubled man ("He fought a war against his will") who slips into a polished pew of a church who is confronted with the same personal address in the Chorus. Just as relevant, just as powerful. The Bridge contains the payoff: we all share the cup. Wonderful crafting by friend, co-writer, Joel Lindsey.

Worship

"Here I am Lord" by Dan Schutte (recorded by James Kilbane and others) is a rare example of Roles applied to a worship setting. V1 starts in the voice of God ("I the Lord of sea and sky") before in the Pre-Chorus asking a question ("whom shall I send?"). The Chorus then (unusually) steps into the first person with the title and the response to that question ("Here I am, Lord") and a promise ("I will go, Lord"). V2 is back in the voice of God but extends the plot in V1 to reveal more of His character ("I have wept," "I will speak my word" etc.) before again asking the question from V1 ("Whom shall I send?").

Musical

"Naughty" from the musical Matilda moves seamlessly through three stories of children/young people stuck in situations they didn't like–from Jack and Jill in V1 to Romeo and Juliet in V2 and Cinderella in V3. The Chorus elegantly responds to each situation, saying you don't have to just grin and bear it, even if you're little. The Bridge contains the payoff before getting back to the title ("if you're stuck in your story... sometimes you have to be a little bit naughty"). Lovely.

"Summer Nights" from Grease uses a different format–cleverly weaving two different roles in every Verse with two very different voices and contrasting points of view of a summer romance.

Jazz

"Let's Call The Whole Thing Off" by Ella Fitzgerald and Louis Armstrong–a classic Gershwin song–takes a different approach to Roles by using narrative to switch between roles ("You say XX, I say YY"). An extended Intro sets up the whole idea effectively ("Our romance is growing flat"). V1 launches into the differences between the two people, in turn, taking differences in pronunciation initially (check out the fun spellings in the lyric sheet!) before going into likes and dislikes. The B section elegantly sets up the tension that is the payoff ("If we call the whole thing off then we must part [...] will break my heart"). Great writing.

Exercise

If you have a copy of the Song Maps Workbook, this would be a good time to complete Exercise #6 – Roles.

Map 6 - Twist

The Twist is one of the most challenging Song Maps to execute successfully, but when it's done well, it is incredibly rewarding, often delivering a spectacular "WOW" moment.

There are two reasons why it's more challenging:

- We need to search hard for words, phrases or plot ideas that create a compelling twist at the same time as retaining the authenticity of the idea and staying true to the genre.
- If a genuine common thread can't be traced through the whole song, there is a risk the Twist could sound contrived, cheesy or just plain funny!

The Twist is great for genres that rely on a strong traditionally-crafted lyric (Country, Southern Gospel, Musicals or Jazz). Applying the Twist to genres with more conversational lyrics (Pop or Worship) would need the twist to be more subtle. However, examples of Twist exist in all genres.

The benefits of pioneering with this Map is that when the word or phrase twist arrives, it's nearly always a memorable moment for the listener and the artist alike. Perhaps the reason we don't see a lot of them is a function of how challenging they are to both find and write, as well as it being a riskier song to pitch to artists.

But I'd encourage you to persevere, because when they are delivered to an artist or A&R as a well-crafted song, they almost always get fast-tracked.

A great source of potential word twist titles is homophones (words that sound the same but have different meanings and spellings), which you can find at www.homophone.com. They list wonderful sound-alike words like:

- Toad/towed/toed
- Ayes/eyes/aes
- Cashing/caching

But I would be careful about using homophones unless you want to write a deliberately funny song (and there's nothing wrong with that!).

There are two types of Twist:

1. A word or phrase twist that uses either a word or phrase in more than one way (more common).
2. A plot twist that introduces a radical change in the development of the song creating a moment of surprise that either resolves or entirely changes the meaning of what has been sung before.

I love both of these techniques because they are very clever. In this book, I am going to focus primarily on a word or phrase twist, because, even in its subtlest form, it is the most useful.

I once wrote a song called "Before Christ" with my wonderful friend and co-writer Sue C Smith in which we extracted three meanings out of the same title, set up by two short Verses and a two-line Bridge. The three meanings were:

1. A long time ago (before Christ = B.C.)
2. A place (before Christ = in heaven)
3. An act of worship (before Christ = bowing before Christ)

The key for us making the Chorus work was to make it very simple:

Title
Title
Another line
Title

And the other line was a very generic but still meaningful "What a world of difference."

But there are many ways you can go about crafting a Twist lyric. Often it's about waiting for the right idea to fall in your path and, when it does, being quick to recognize it and capture it.

What does the Twist look like?

The Twist Map below applies to a word or phrase twist. This simply sets up the title (the word or phrase of the twist) from two or more perspectives in each of the Verses. To deliver this requires some thought as to how to set up the twist when it arrives in the Chorus.

The neat thing about this Map is that given the very different approaches to the same word or phrase, we know that the Chorus will be "recolored" with each Verse, helping to move the lyric forward with each section.

The Twist can be represented as follows:

How to use the Twist

My suggestion for working with a word or phrase twist would be to approach it as follows:

1. Find a word or phrase that can mean different things in different contexts or circumstances. For effective use of a word or phrase twist in anything other than a humorous song, my suggestion would be to make it a subtle but effective change in meaning–not subtle enough and it could potentially backfire.
2. As with other Maps, decide on the exact title and the central idea for the Chorus. In writing the Chorus, you may need to sacrifice some detail to make it work for the two or three different ways of approaching the title to achieve a compelling twist. Repetition is a neat way of making the Chorus work in a variety of contexts.
3. Decide what should be the first meaning of the word or phrase. How does that idea develop to lead eventually to the Chorus idea? This is V1.
4. Decide what should be the second meaning of the word or phrase. Again, how does that idea develop to lead to the Chorus idea? How does it differ from V1? Once you are happy, this is V2.
5. The Bridge (the payoff) can work in any number of ways. For example, it can point to a common thread in both meanings of the twist. It can summarize what it all means. Or it can go to a whole new place. As long as it somehow gets us back to the Chorus.

Example of a Twist writable idea

Writable idea: "Free"

Verse 1 – Approach 1

Prodigal son, having spent my inheritance I only deserve to be a servant in my Father's house. But instead, I am...

Chorus – Title

Free (i.e. Not a servant)
Free

Verse 2 – Approach 2

Christ has settled my debt, paid the price. His grace isn't cheap but it's

Chorus – Title

Free (i.e. I don't have to pay for it)
Free

Bridge – Payoff

Free from X or Y, but also free to choose to serve Him

Chorus – Title

Free (i.e. Free from my issues to serve Him)
Free

Example of a Twist lyric

Building on the writable idea above, here's a draft SoGo lyric to demonstrate the Twist Map.

Lyric: "Free"

Verse 1
How can I stand here
So undeserving
A prodigal son
Who's come back home
It's hard to believe
I'm no longer a slave
But Father, You see me as Your own
And I'm...

Chorus
Free
Free
Now I'm alive
And with tears in my eyes
I am free
Free
Cause You've given so generously
I am Free

Verse 2
Now as I can stand here
In the arms of my Savior

You settled my debt
Nailed to a tree
So freely You've given
So my sin is broken
You paid the price
But Your grace isn't cheap
It is...

Chorus

Bridge
I'm free from my selfishness
Free from despair
Free from the heavy chains
That held me back there
Free to see hope
In all that I do
Free to choose love
And I choose to serve You, now I'm

Chorus

Some points I'd make:

1. The chorus needs to work with both meanings, so simplicity and repetition can help here. It's also articulating a new place (after meaning 1) which is helpful in moving the lyric forward.
2. The function of each Verse is to build two separate contexts to make the Chorus mean something different after each section, but still moving the same plot forward.
3. It's important that both ideas (for Verse 1 and Verse 2) are individually substantial enough.
4. It's also important that the sequence of ideas helps move the song forward in a logical progression, e.g., from dark to light, from time one to time two, etc.
5. You may well have spotted that there's also a plot twist in the Bridge: because I am free I want to serve You. This can be a cool way of achieving a payoff.

Variations on the Twist

In some ways, the Twist Map is one of the most flexible in that the Map needs to serve the nature of the twist that you are working with. For example, if the word or phrase twist is best set up as the title (as in Julie Roberts' "Men and Mascara"), then that's the best place to put it. The benefit of putting it in the title is that it's likely to get repeated, thereby reminding everyone what a genius lyric it is.

On the other hand, if the twist is a plot twist, which requires a story to develop before it can twist into something else (as in the UK's 1976 winning entry for the Eurovision Song Contest by Brotherhood of Man,"Kisses for Me", which leaves the twist until the very last line) then obviously the Map reflects that.

Commercial examples of using the Twist

Great examples of Twist include:

Country

"God's Will" by Martina McBride–a brilliant lyric written around a title that was begging to be written. V1 introduces the little boy with a smile on his face and braces on his legs ("God's Will" meaning 1). The Chorus sets up the title so sweetly ("searching for...God's Will"). V2 continues to develop the story, ending in little Will's prayers for everybody except for himself. V3 really nails the phrase twist, with the singer saying she found God's Will ("God's Will" meaning 2) on a note little Will had written: "Me and God love you." Sweet, touching and effective.

"Men and Mascara" by Julie Roberts–I love this song because it's not only clever, but the AABA song form and short Verses make it get right to the point. After some brilliantly thought-out images ("empty bottle of wine on the hardwood floor") and metaphors ("black rivers running down her face") the twist is repeated at the end of each Verse in the refrain: "men and mascara ALWAYS RUN." Fantastic.

Pop

"It's a Beautiful Day" by Michael Bublé–great example of a plot twist. V1 starts off telling us how he's been dumped by his girlfriend, then, just before the Chorus hits us with the twist in the plot: he's happy about it! ("When you said goodbye my whole world shines.") V2 goes on–elements of Tension/Response here–to tell us what his newfound freedom is like before the Outro summing up the whole idea ("Any day that you're gone away it's a beautiful day"). Not what we might have thought from either the title or the beginning of V1. But that's what happens in the Twist.

CCM

"Satisfied" by Ronnie Freeman–a beautiful song written with my friend and co-writer Tony Wood. V1 sets up the reasons for the singer to be satisfied ("each breath I breathe," "color the skies," "provide for my needs" etc.). The Chorus is half response, half declaration before twisting the title of the song along with a lovely double setup rhyme ("plea," "be") and prayer ("that You're satisfied with me"). Fabulous writing.

Southern Gospel

"Under Cross Examination" by Brian Free and Assurance–a song that totally commits to the Judgment Day metaphor and uses every Verse to support it until the very last line, "I rest my case." Brilliant. Here, writers Steve Marshall, Ed Stivers and Marty Funderburk delivered a work of SoGo genius.

Worship

"Above All" by Lenny Leblanc sung by Randy Travis, Michael W Smith, and others. Lovely writing for so many reasons, a classic worship song that gives us a beautiful phrase twist at the end of the Chorus. V1 and V2 sung as a double first Verse set the title up firmly to mean one thing–that God is above all things. The Chorus, which includes the lovely simile "Like a rose trampled on the ground" then nails the twist at the end: "you thought of me... ABOVE ALL." Big cheer for spectacular crafting from one of my favorite worship writers.

Musical

"For Good" from the musical Wicked–some of the best crafting of lyrics can be found in musicals because they have to move the plot forward. This is a lovely use of a phrase twist to nail a song's title as well as it hitting a touching moment in the musical. V1 and V2 develop the two characters singing this duet, confirming the positive impact each one has on the other. The Chorus cleverly builds toward the twist, establishing by the end of the song that they have both been changed for good, meaning changed for the better AND changed forever. Brilliant work.

See also "The Hammer" from the musical Matilda for a variation involving one big figurative lyric.

Jazz

Shirley Bassey's "Big Spender" is an excellent example of the kind of subtle word twist I was talking about earlier, taking one word and making it mean something different with a contraction or extension, relevant and cool ("Hey Big Spender, spend a little time with me"). The Map doesn't totally fit as well to this song versus other songs, but if you take the last two lines (the Refrain) as being a substitute for the Chorus and you have V1 building the meaning of what "Big Spender" is before the refrain delivers the punchline. The Big Spender is spending MONEY and spending TIME. No V2 but the B section sells the idea in the Refrain a little more before repeating V1. Cool crafting of a minimalistic classic.

"I Got It Bad (And That Ain't Good)" by Ella Fitzgerald is a great example of a different kind of twist, an idea twist rather than a word or phase twist, using opposites. Great approach.

Exercise

If you have a copy of the Song Maps Workbook, this would be a good time to complete Exercise #7 – Twist.

Map 7 - Literal/Figurative

Our final Map is Literal/Figurative, which is also a great Map for telling stories.

Literal/Figurative is fascinating because, although it's one of the most challenging to get right, it is potentially one of the most powerful Maps.

If you think back to the stories that you remember from your childhood–Aesop's fables, the parables of Jesus in the Bible, CS Lewis–these are all works that have stood the test of time. And the same techniques that gave these works their longevity are available to us today.

I say it's among the most challenging Song Maps to get right because it really does need an effective, rock-solid, watertight metaphor or simile to make it work. The risk you run, therefore, is that if the chosen figurative language proves not to be effective, your lyric could fall down. But it's all totally doable.

So I'd encourage you to give this a try because, while it might be a bit more challenging, the rewards are so great. Once you have mastered this Map, the quality of your writing will go up exponentially.

Just to remind us:

- **Literal language** uses words or phrases to state facts as they are. It paints a picture of the physical or emotional place the singer is singing from.
- **Figurative language** uses words or phrases to

> mean something different from their literal meaning and includes metaphor, simile, personification, hyperbole, or symbolism.

Given its ability to paint wonderful pictures, Literal/Figurative can be used in all genres of music. However, some of the best examples can be found in Country, Southern Gospel, Pop and Musicals and Jazz.

What does Literal/Figurative look like?

The exact pattern of Literal/Figurative can take a variety of forms. Of course, figurative language is an essential part of the lyricist's tool kit and can appear as a thread throughout all songs. The difference here is that Literal/Figurative is used to assign ideas to entire song sections at a time.

Literal/Figurative can be represented as follows:

How to use Literal/Figurative

Note that this Map can be used in two ways: literal/figurative and figurative/literal. The decision is yours. However, for this book, I'm assuming the former.

In working with Literal/Figurative you might like to consider the following:

1. As with other Maps, decide on your title and idea for the Chorus first. If your V1 is going to be literal, then the Chorus is the time to focus on exactly what about the literal V1 is the focus of the song.
2. How does the situation look literally? Paint a picture, the more "furniture," or descriptions of concrete objects, the better. Explore all your senses. Show the listener what this literal place looks like. How does this place lead to your Chorus? This is your V1.
3. How does the situation look figuratively? What effective metaphor or simile helps enhance the picture painted in V1? How effective is the metaphor or simile? How does this lead to your Chorus? This is your V2.
4. What is the payoff or conclusion? How does this relate to the listener? What do the literal and figurative situations in V1 and V2 mean? Is there a life lesson to be learned? How does this lead back to the Chorus? This is your Bridge.

Example of a Literal/Figurative writable idea

Writable idea: "You're An Angel"

Verse 1 - Literal
Picture of you in the summer sun
Warm smiles, love being here with you

Chorus - Title

You're an angel
When did you come down?
You're an angel

Verse 2 - figurative
A long way from heaven
Golden glow, halo, light
Flutter of wings don't fly away

Chorus
You're an angel
When did you come down?
You're an angel

Bridge - Payoff
You bring the angel out in me

Chorus
You're an angel
When did you come down?
You're an angel

Example of a Literal/Figurative lyric

Here's a lyric to demonstrate Literal/Figurative using the above writable idea.

Lyric: "You're An Angel"

Verse 1

Your hair glows in the summer sun
The golden girl to everyone
Your smile can warm the coldest winter's night
And when you whisper in my ear
You breathe out a piece of heaven here
And when you laugh I'm almost hypnotized, 'cuz

Chorus
You're an angel
An angel
When did you come down?
You're an angel
An angel
Surely there's no doubt
You're an angel

Verse 2
I'm so far from heaven's Throne
But you paint me with your golden glow
A little bit of halo goes a long, long way
I love the love, the light you bring
I hope you have no angel wings
Just promise me, you'll never fly away, 'cause

Chorus

Bridge
For every shade of beautiful I see

The more you bring the angel out in me

Chorus

Some points I'd make:

1. While the structure is Literal/Figurative, there is no reason to leave out effective figurative language in V1, especially if it signals the figurative theme that is about to come in the Chorus/V2.
2. The impact of the Bridge building on the metaphor already set up but also inserting a twist–helps to provide some cohesion for the lyric.
3. Note that to introduce a different metaphor in this lyric would feel awkward, having committed to the "angel" pictures previously. It's sensible, for the sake of clarity and unity of the lyric, to stick with one figurative picture in this Map.

Variations on Literal/Figurative

We've already talked about literal and figurative sections being swapped around (i.e. V1 figurative, V2 literal). It's possible to assign Literal/Figurative in other ways.

- Another variation is as in Dierks Bentley's "I Hold On", which uses figurative in the Verses and literal in the Chorus.
- Michael Bolton's "Love is a Wonderful Thing" has the first few lines of each Verse use literal language and the second half of each Verse use figurative language.

The main distinction between simply using figurative language as a tool and this Song Map is that the use of the figurative is structural rather than just applying it in an isolated or unsystematic way.

Commercial examples of Literal/Figurative

Wonderful examples of Literal/Figurative I'd highlight include:

Country

"Peter Pan" by Kelsey Ballerini–one of those songs you hear and immediately wish you had written, projecting the qualities of a children's story onto a hopeless boyfriend. V1 starts with the literal, painting the picture of how the boyfriend let her down before the Pre-Chorus introduces figurative elements of the Peter Pan story ("lost boy," "head up in the clouds"). The Chorus continues to build the metaphor ("always going to fly away," "no such place as Neverland," "never grow up to be a man") before nailing the title with a rhyme setup: "Peter Pan." V2 introduces more elements of the Pan story ("too good to be true," "wanted to believe in you," "happily ever never"). The Bridge includes a lovely phrase twist: from Peter Pan being a lost boy in the Pre-Choruses to the line "I know who you are, You don't know what you lost, boy...too busy chasing stars". Fabulous crafting.

Other Country examples of Literal/Figurative include"I Hold On" by Dierks Bentley and "The Dance" by Garth Brooks.

Pop

"Love Is A Wonderful Thing" by Michael Bolton is a good example of Literal/Figurative, only the structure is a little different: it contains both literal and figurative in V1 and in V2, starting with the figurative and ending on the literal ("Birds fly, sun shines, same applies to you and I"). The Chorus is the title. V2 is another metaphor ("only thing a river knows is running to the sea"). The Bridge extends this mix of nature and love ("when the cold wind blows, you'll be there to warm me").

CCM

"Life Means So Much" by Chris Rice–two figurative Verses: V1, "life is a journal page," Chorus is "life means so much," V2, "life is a bank account for us to spend." The Bridge delivers a lovely payoff: "we can prove the value of life by giving it away." Excellent work, Chris.

Also, "Diamonds" by Hawk Nelson is a good example of this Map, but in a Figurative/Literal format.

Southern Gospel

"God Will Close the Door" by Brian Free and Assurance–V1 starts with the figurative, of when God closed the door to the ark to protect Noah and the animals. Chorus is the title: "God will close the door." V2 is talking about me: "I've seen God open and close doors and I'm grateful for both." The Bridge is the payoff: when He closes it, He locks it and "throws away the key" to totally protect me. Thanks to my co-writers Sue C Smith and Kenna West for that one.

Worship

"Waterfall" by Chris Tomlin–V1 sets the literal tension ("I seek You, I thirst for You") followed by a transition in the Pre-Chorus ("You're an ocean to my soul"). Chorus is the figurative simile ("Your love is like a waterfall raining down on me"). V2 is more figurative, a metaphor ("In this dry and desert land / lead me to streams of mercy"). Bridge extends the original simile ("coming like a flood, I'm dancing in the rain / rivers of grace"). Unusual to have so much figurative in one song of this genre, but it still works.

Musical

"Love And The Weather" from White Christmas–some brilliant crafting here by one of the masters, Irving Berlin. Intro starts to list common characteristics of both love and the weather (unpredictable, irresponsible, unbelievable, unreliable). Double V1 mixes the figurative and literal, making comparisons before the B section, which continues the combination of literal and figurative with the consequences of love being like the weather ("love walked out [...] into a storm"). As you'd expect, some fabulous rhymes and great economy of words, but still makes good use of the Literal/Figurative technique.

Jazz

"Cheek to Cheek" by Louis Armstrong and Ella Fitzgerald has some lovely Literal/Figurative language in a slightly different structure of the Map applied to an AABA song form. V1 starts with two lines of figurative (heaven), coming to the literal by the end of the Verse (dancing cheek to cheek). Same format for V2. The B section launches into more figurative, liking dancing cheek to cheek more than climbing a mountain or going fishing. An extended B section then returns to the literal ("I want my arms about you"). Enchanting.

Exercise

If you have a copy of the Song Maps Workbook, this would be a good time to complete Exercise #8 - Literal/figurative.

Summary

In this chapter, we've looked at seven universal Song Maps, what they look like and how to use them. We've seen examples of using each Map to create a writable idea and a draft lyric. We've also talked about variations and seen the many and varied uses of each Map across all genres of lyric-driven songs in commercial songwriting.

The next chapter is important. I'll show you where to find more Maps for yourself, how to combine two or more Song Maps in one lyric and how to apply them to other song forms before talking about some advanced Song Mapping techniques.

6 WHAT NEXT?

Congratulations! You now have:

- An understanding of the benefits of writing with Song Maps
- An understanding of what to do when ideas come at any moment during the day or night
- The "songwriter's secret weapon" to writing moving lyrics
- A four-step process to start writing with Song Maps
- Seven Song Maps to apply to your writing
- An approach to writing with each Song Map
- The foundation to start building your Idea Bank of writable ideas and, if you have completed the exercises in the Song Map Workbook, you have seven writable ideas to take into your next writing session or co-write.

In this chapter, I want to give you some ideas about what to do next: where to find more Maps for yourself, how to combine or alter Song Maps, and how to apply them to different song forms. Finally, I'll talk about some advanced Song Mapping techniques. If you are following along with the Workbook, by the end of this chapter you will have an extra five Song Maps to work with. Enjoy!

Where to find more Song Maps?

Song Maps can be found everywhere you hear a song. Whether you're driving down the freeway listening to the radio, shopping with muzak in the background, killing it in the gym to a stirring tune or worshiping at your church. As long as there is a lyric, there is a Map of some sort.

I loved reading Austin Kleon's book Steal Like an Artist, in which he says,

---

> "Every artist gets asked the question, 'Where do you get your ideas?' The honest artist says, 'I steal them.'"
>
> AUSTIN KLEON

He also quotes the late David Bowie, saying,

> "The only art I'll ever study is stuff that I can steal from."
>
> DAVID BOWIE

I totally relate to that. As a family, we love vacationing in Italy. I remember us once visiting Florence to look at the fabulous pieces at art museums and galleries such as the Uffizi, the Brancacci Chapel, the Pitti Palace and so much more. While the colors, the artistry and the stories behind the art were compelling and inspiring in themselves, I remember most the lessons I took away for writing songs. Lessons about perspective, light and shade, themes, focus, and passion.

Song Mapping is a way of "stealing like an artist" in your lyric writing without anyone knowing.

However, this comes with a health warning: mapping the lyrics of the songs you love can sometimes totally ruin your enjoyment of them. And this happens to me a lot. While I still love the songs, Song Maps help me understand more about why I love them–maybe for the melody, harmonies, the idea behind the lyric (even though it could be crafted better) or maybe the artistry of the artist. But you should not be surprised if you start looking at some of your all-time favorites in a different way after Mapping them because sometimes, or maybe even often, the development of songs we hear fail to deliver a good payoff or have a mappable lyric development

So, the big question is:

"Where can we find more Maps that will improve our writing?"

The best chances are always going to be lyric-driven genres of songs. For example, out of the 31-odd categories at the 2016 Grammy Awards, only a dozen or so categories would be relevant to lyric writers (some like Arranging and Packaging are not at all relevant to studying the craft of lyric writing). Out of those, my personal ranking as potential sources for Song Maps would be as follows:

- Country
- Gospel/Contemporary Christian Music (CCM)
- Pop
- Rap
- Rock
- R&B
- Alternative
- American Roots

In Mapping a song that you think is potentially "Mappable," the process is simple. In fact, it's very similar to the process we went through for generating a writable idea:

1. Write down the structure of the song
2. Summarize in a few phrases exactly what each section says
3. Extract (or Map) the significance of each section

This will quickly give you many new Song Maps you can start working with. If you can't find an identifiable Map in the lyric don't worry–just move on to another song until you find one.

Exercise

If you have a copy of the Song Maps Workbook, this would be a good time to complete Exercise #9 - Find Additional Maps.

How to combine two Song Maps

I'm sure you realize by now that not all songs need to be written according to the seven Song Maps set out in this book. Indeed, the aim of this book is not to prescribe a set format for every song but to provide a starting point to help writers write their best work. As you integrate Song Maps into your writing, you will soon develop a set of Maps you feel most comfortable with.

My working set currently stands at around 30 Song Maps, some of which are specific to certain genres, some of which are very general. One way to generate alternatives to boost your own set of Maps is by combining Maps.

For example, take the basic Tension/Response and combine it with Places, resulting in this:

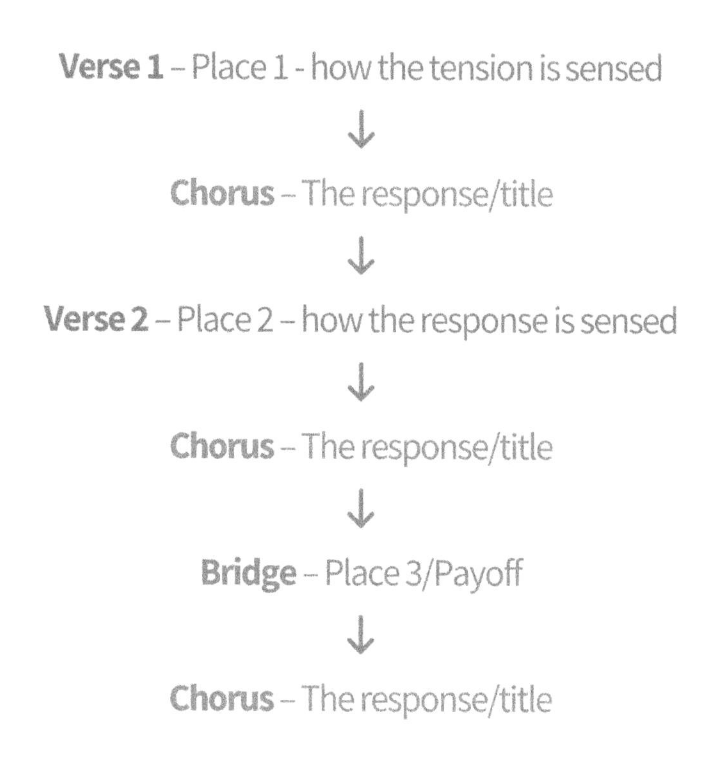

As you can see, the combination of two Maps has the impact of significantly strengthening the development of the song, since two forces are working to move the plot forward.

A great example of this is Keith Urban's "Days Go By", which moves geographically (V1 driving on the interstate, V2 out on the roof), moves in time (V1 now, V2 the other night) as well as following a Tension/Response format. All of this movement reinforces the whole point of the song, neatly summed up in the Bridge ("We think about tomorrow then it slips away / We talk about forever but we've only got today"). Great crafting.

As another example: if you look back at my lyric to "When You Lose Your Dad," the Map is a combination of Timezones and Places.

Writing with a combination of Song Maps is very simple:

- Decide which Song Maps you would like to combine
- Select your song structure (e.g., AABA or VCVCBC)
- Assign to each section an element from your selected Song Maps
- Review to make sure your new Song Map has effective development and payoff

It may take a few attempts to get it right, but this is a neat way of generating new and unique Song Maps to reflect better your authentic voice in your own writing, much like a professional keyboard player creates their own patches on a synthesizer, rather than using factory patches.

Exercise

If you have a copy of the Song Maps Workbook, this would be a good time to complete Exercise #10 - Combining Two Song Maps.

Altering a Song Map

Altering a Song Map can be just as rewarding as combining Song Maps. As I said earlier in this book, all we are doing in the process of Song Mapping is assigning ideas to song sections to make sure the lyric moves forward.

It's therefore very simple to modify a Song Map with a totally new element, which is not necessarily part of the original (or any other) Song Map. What is critical, however, is that any new element introduced has the impact of moving the plot forward. In other words, for a VCVCBC structure,

- Wherever we were in V1, the Chorus needs to move us to a new place
- Wherever we were in the Chorus, V2 needs to move us to a new place
- Etc.

For example, Taylor Swift's song "Shake It Off" from her Grammy-winning album 1989 was brilliantly crafted by writers Swift, Martin and Shellback around a variation of Problem/Declaration: Instead of writing Problem/Declaration/Response they write Perception/Declaration/Reality.

In this format, they move the lyric from what people think in V1 to the declaration (also a response) in the Chorus to setting out reality in V2.

Altering a Song Map can not only introduce fresh elements into the Song Map, but it can also be an effective way to help develop the lyric and move the story on. Examples of fresh elements that can be introduced into a Song Map include:

- States of mind (historical, now, future)
- Times
- Generations
- Fears, hopes, aspirations, reality
- What I've done, what I will do now
- Signal what's coming, my response to knowing what's coming
- Knowing, telling
- The lesson
- The solution
- The conclusion (meaning)
- How I feel about the lesson/solution/conclusion
- Remembering
- The future
- Eternity
- Everything's going to turn out alright

Any of these could be applied to any section of a song to provide some fresh perspective for the lyric.

Exercise

If you have a copy of the Song Maps Workbook, this would be a good time to complete Exercise #11 - Altering a Song Map.

What about other song forms?

While we have spent most of the time in this book working with a generic song form–VCVCBC–Song Maps can certainly be applied to other song forms. For example,

- AAA – substitute the Refrain for the Chorus
- AABA – similarly, substitute the Refrain for the Chorus
- VCVC – incorporate the function of the Bridge (e.g., Payoff) into the end of V2 or even Pre-Chorus 2
- VVCVCBC – use V1 and V2 to articulate the V1 idea of the Song Map

While these are the main song forms we tend to work with in commercial songwriting, there are times when the song form can be driven by idea development. Examples of this can be found in modern Worship songs or hymns where V1 and V2 are simply repeating the same lyric with an anthemic Chorus, which leads into an Outro or Bridge, which in turn drives home the central message of the lyric.

It is, therefore, worth experimenting with this. While we are somewhat pre-programmed to expect the traditional song forms above, it is entirely possible that the emotional impact of a well-crafted lyric written in (and served well by) a non-traditional song form could potentially serve your song better.

Exercise

If you have a copy of the Song Maps Workbook, this would be a good time to complete Exercise #12 - Other Song Forms.

Advanced Song Mapping

You could argue that combining and altering Song Maps is advanced Song Mapping. However, there are a few more nuances I wanted to mention here.

Pre-Chorus Mapping

While it's possible to assign ideas to the main song sections, it's also possible to assign ideas to sub-sections. For example, the function of a Pre Chorus is very different from that of a Chorus or a Verse. So it can sometimes be very helpful to assign a specific idea to Pre-Choruses to ensure an effective and natural flow of a lyric each time we get to a Chorus.

Bridge Mapping

In all the Maps in Chapter 5, I have included the Bridge as an essential part of the Map. In reality, not all songs need a Bridge. If you do write one, a Bridge is a great opportunity to go somewhere very different before returning to the central idea in the Chorus. A Bridge can be very short or quite long; it can hit a new register for the singer or be a very quiet moment for the song.

While I have suggested elements for a Bridge in each of the Maps outlined in Chapter 5, if you are following the four-step process for writing with Song Maps, once you have your writable idea sketched out you may want to take a moment to make sure your Bridge is serving your song the best way possible. It could be that, by taking it somewhere very different, you might make that payoff a lot more effective.

Outro Mapping

Not every song has or even needs a lyrical Outro. By this, I'm not talking about ad-libs or throw away lines as part of the production but lyrical content that is essential to the storyline of the lyric.

So, if your song does need an Outro (e.g., "When You Lose Your Dad"), it is important to make sure that it serves a purpose in moving the lyric forward or delivering a payoff.

Summary

In this chapter, I have discussed where to find more Song Maps, how to apply Song Maps to different song forms, how to combine and alter Song Maps and some advanced Song Mapping techniques.

In the next chapter I will send you off with some final thoughts to help you along the way.

Exercise

If you have a copy of the Song Maps Workbook, this would be a good time to complete the last three exercises:

- Exercise #13–Advanced Song Mapping
- Exercise #14–The Songwriter's Secret Weapon
- Exercise #15–Create Your Writable Idea Bank

7 OUTRO

With this book I've tried to pass on a writing technique I discovered many years ago that completely transformed the way I write lyrics. I hope and pray that it will be as useful to you as it has been and continues to be for me.

In this chapter I want to take a different perspective: if you're writing a particular genre of song, what Map should you start with? I then run through some final thoughts about the craft before signing off and giving you my contact information.

But first, just for a bit of fun, I'd like to demonstrate how Song Maps can help you write ANY title–even an impossible title.

Writing an impossible title

I promised earlier that I'll show you how to write an impossible title. In reality, once you've got to grips with Song Maps, you will find it easy to write literally ANY title–everything on the spectrum of writability, from impossible, totally unwritable titles to totally writable always-going-to-work titles.

At the beginning of my teaching classes (which are sometimes called "Lyric Strategies–How to write ANY title") I ask my students for six titles–three highly writable titles and three impossible titles. At the end of the class, we apply Song Maps to each one of them. And it's a lot of fun finding places all of these titles can go, especially the impossible ones.

Here's an impossible title my wife thought up:

"Ironing Forever."

It's difficult to see how that title could result in a song that could catapult a writer into the Music Hall of Fame. But that's exactly the point, it's a difficult title to write and let's see where it can go.

So, just as an exercise, here's how I'd turn that impossible title into a writable idea by applying Tension/Response to it.

Writable idea: "Ironing Forever"

Verse 1 – How the tension is sensed
Piles of freshly-washed, wrinkled clothes on
the floor
Treading on my best shirt on the way to the
bathroom
How I hate that after all the washing there's
still more work to do
I've no energy to get out the ironing board

And I'm so slow I'll be...

Chorus – The response
Ironing forever
Ironing forever
I have better things to do with my life, than
Ironing forever

Verse 2 – How the solution is sensed
I'd like to twitch my nose and it all be gone
I'd love to upload it to www.upwork.com and get it back done
Or hire a housekeeper to sort it out (and all the other things waiting for her)
But in the end it's easier to
Just take it to my Mum, who's been...

Chorus – The response
Ironing forever
Ironing forever
I have better things to do with my life, than
Ironing forever

Bridge – How I feel about the solution
She folds my shirts just the way I like them to fit my drawer
She even irons my handkerchiefs, ties and underwear
She's got all the sprays, the starch and stuff

And a heavy duty iron that will go on, and on,
and on, and on
That's why she doesn't mind...

Chorus – The response
Ironing forever
Ironing forever
I have better things to do with my life, than
Ironing forever

Like I said in Chapter 4, while I honestly believe you can write ANY title with Song Maps, not all titles make great lyrics!

But on a serious note, if you find yourself having trouble with any of the exercises in the Workbook, you might like to try writing an impossible title, just as an exercise. It's sometimes easier to bed down the principles in this book in an unpressured writing environment. You never know, your title might just have a lot more scope than you might have first thought!

So what Map do I start with?

While the seven Song Maps included in this book represent a selection of universal Song Maps that you can immediately use in your writing, you may be wondering which one to start with.

Earlier in this book I suggested that Tension/Response is the Swiss Army knife of Song Maps because it is by far the simplest and most intuitive to apply. That will almost always be a great place to start.

One of the reasons for selecting these seven Song Maps is I believe all of them can be used in every genre of lyric-driven songwriting. However, there are certain Maps that tend to get used more often than others in particular genres.

Having listened to thousands of songs in researching this book and analyzed which songs are most used, here are my top-3 recommendations for which Song Map you might like to start with for each genre of lyric-driven songs:

Country

1. Timezones

2. Roles

3. Places

Classics like Randy Travis' "Three Wooden Crosses" and Kenny Rogers' "Coward of the County" are great templates. The storytelling nature of Timezones, Roles and Places clearly means they work well for Country Songs.

With hits like "Hell Yeah," "Roll With Me" and "Lucky Man," Montgomery Gentry gets my vote for the Master of the Roles Map!

Pop

1. Problem/Declaration

2. Tension/Response

3.Other

No surprises here. "Other" includes Song Maps that I have not covered in this book, such as Gradual Reveal. If you'd be interested in learning more about that or other Maps, I'd value your feedback–just email me at the contact details at the end of the book.

CCM

1.Tension/Response

2.Problem/Declaration

3.Timezones

Again, no surprises here. Tension/Response is so appropriate for the "therapy" nature of CCM, which often describes the internal/external struggles associated with the Christian walk.

Southern Gospel

1.Problem/Declaration

2.Tension/Response

3.Timezones

Similar to CCM but the inspirational nature of many Southern Gospel songs lends itself so readily to Problem/Declaration. But don't forget the more story-telling Maps like Places and Roles because they work brilliantly too.

Worship

1.Problem/Declaration

2.Truth/Declaration

3.Gratitude/Declaration

Problem/Declaration does lend itself to Worship writing (e.g., Matt Redman's "Holy," Hillsong's "Cornerstone" and "Oceans"). Truth/Declaration is very similar in structure but starts with a Biblical truth before a declarative "Praise" moment (e.g., Chris Tomlin's "How Great is Our God" and "Jesus Messiah" and Benton Brown's "Everlasting God"). Gratitude/Declaration is also a strong variation on the Problem/Declaration Map (e.g., Matt Redman's "Blessed Be Your Name" and Chris Tomlin's "Amazing Grace (My Chains Fell Off)").

Musical

1.Problem/Declaration

2.Roles

3.Tension/Response

By definition the lyrics of songs in a musical need to move the overall plot of the show forward, so it is no surprise that we find some very strong writing in this genre of music. The fact that the quality of songs has the power to determine whether a musical is a hit or a miss means they often attract the best writing talent. Think of the costs involved in making a film like Frozen and it's easy to see why songs like "Let It Go" are great examples of the songwriting craft.

Jazz

1.Tension/Response

2.Places

3.Timezones

Again, we find some very strong writing in classic jazz.

Some final comments

As I said earlier, in researching this book, I've listened to thousands of songs. In picking them apart, analyzing them and trying to figure out what makes them succeed or just suck, I have heard some spectacular songs that have not only moved me to tears, but they have reminded me of the power of a song and its ability to totally reframe my reality. For me, the process of writing this book has underscored the importance of not just writing songs, but writing the very best songs we can write.

While I'm a huge fan of co-writing, it's amazing what you can write when you are looking to write the very best song, rather than the best song you can write in three hours. So lately, I've been writing a whole load more on my own, just to give myself some space to play, to be moved and not so driven with my writing. And this approach has yielded some of my more significant successes in terms of external recognition and awards. But I still love co-writing and solo writing and will continue to do both.

Now that you have seen Song Maps in action, I genuinely hope you will find them an important addition to your crafting tools, whether you're writing on your own or with a co-writer.

There are so many facets to this craft and calling, in many ways, I still feel I've only just scratched the surface. One small concern I have, now that this book is published, is that if my co-writers read this, they might have unrealistic expectations for the ideas I bring to our writing sessions! We are all learning. And I'm no exception! But I'll have to deal with that!

As with all things to do with the craft of songwriting, there is nothing cast in stone about this technique–if 100% of it works for you, brilliant. If parts of it don't work for you, then maybe focus on those parts that do. At the end of the day, the aim is not to write a song the right way but to write the right song. And to enjoy the journey.

So, as this final chapter draws to an end, I'd like to leave you with two thoughts:

Firstly, thank you for giving me your time. If you have read this book and completed all the exercises in the Workbook,

YOU ARE A TOTAL ROCK STAR
You deserve that Grammy!

But no matter how deep into this book you've been able to dive, my hope and prayer is for your songs to shine and for them to be discovered and used. I hope this book somehow helps to unlock them.

Second, I would love to hear about your successes with the tools and techniques you have learned about in this book. If you meet me at a seminar please talk to me! If you are in one of my open critique sessions, warn me if your song is about to hit me with the songwriter's secret weapon and make me cry! But seriously, if this book has been helpful, I would love to hear from you, so please email me at:

simon@simonhawkins.com

May God bless you, your writing and the extraordinary journey you have ahead of you.

– SJLH.

APPENDIX — RESOURCES

One of the primary motivations for writing this book was that Song Maps are not found in any other publication. Song Mapping is such a powerful process that I would love people to know about it, so please do pass on the information in this book to others you think will benefit.

There are other exceptional resources out there I would recommend if you have not yet found them:

Books

- *Song Maps – A New System to Write Your Best Lyrics* and Audiobook by Simon Hawkins
- *Song Maps Workbook* by Simon Hawkins
- *The Organized Songwriter Workbook* by Simon Hawkins
- *Writing Better Lyrics* by Pat Pattison
- *Songwriting Without Boundaries* by Pat Pattison

- *Popular Lyric Writing* by Andrea Stolpe
- *Beginning Songwriting* by Andrea and Jan Stolpe
- *The Songwriter's Idea Book* by Sheila Davis
- *Successful Lyric Writing* by Sheila Davis
- *The Frustrated Songwriter's Handbook* by Karl Coryat
- *Songwriter's Journal* by Elizabeth Evans

Courses

- SongU.com
- Berklee Music School's Online Programs — particularly: Lyric Writing: Tools and Strategies, Lyric Writing: Writing Lyrics to Music, Lyric Writing: Writing From the Title, and Commercial Songwriting Techniques
- Kingdom Songs University - https://www.kingdomsongsuniversity.com/

Seminars

- Write About Jesus (WAJ) - www.writeaboutjesus.com

Support

- Nashville Songwriters Association International (NSAI) - https://www.nashvillesongwriters.com/
- Nashville Christian Songwriters (NCS) - https://www.nashvillechristiansongwriters.com/

- TAXI - https://www.taxi.com/

Apps:

- Songspace - https://songspace.com/
- Rhymer's Block - https://appsite.skygear.io/rhymer_s_block/
- Word Palette - http://www.wordpalette.io

THANK YOUS

I wish I could mention everyone who has helped me on my journey writing this book, but there simply isn't space. Without a doubt, my incredibly supportive family in England and my 100 wonderful co-writers from all over the world deserve to be listed here.

Special thanks to my wife Sandra, who is not only an amazing wife, mother, and teacher of my three beautiful children, but also a never-ending source of encouragement and common sense. She comes up with the best song ideas (I am not kidding). I wish I could write a book about how she does that.

Thanks to my children, who are an inspiration to me in so many ways they will never realize–to Poppy, who came up with the term "Song Maps" before I did (you are so much more of an author than I am). Monty, who can feel deeply the power of a big ballad like no other 11 year old I know (you have so much music in you). And to Barty, the only 7-year old I know who can rock the Vatican in Rome with his rendition of Figaro (but based on how much practice you get at home, my beautiful boy, I'm not surprised).

Thanks to my mother, Molly Hawkins, who was my #1 fan before I knew what fans were. And to my late Father, Norman Hawkins, who I know would love to have read this book. He would be very happy that the songs he brought home from the US all those years ago inspired me to do anything like this.

Thanks to Sue C Smith and Holly Zabka for signing me to my first staff publishing deal in Nashville at Brentwood-Benson Music Publishing (now Universal/Capitol CMG Publishing). I am so grateful to you. Much of this book is down to the journey on which you helped me take the first few steps.

Thanks also to my wonderful co-writers (I still learn so much from each song we write) and extended family in Nashville and at WAJ, who were guinea pigs for much of the material presented in this book in my Lyric Strategies class. You have given back so much more than you know.

Thanks to Pat Pattison and Andrea Stolpe at Berklee Music School, without whom I would never have gotten signed as a staff songwriter in the first place.

Finally, special thanks also to my exceptional editor Harry Althoff and brilliant designer Ida Fia Sveningsson, who have both been fabulous to work with. Thanks too to Mike Bryant, who has been a brilliant writing buddy. Also, thanks to Chandler, Ramy, Emily and Sean and the rest of my new family at SPS.

Thank you. You are all genuinely awesome people.

ABOUT THE AUTHOR

Simon Hawkins is an award-winning songwriter, producer, and Amazon best-selling author, based on the south coast of England.

In 2004, Simon became a full-time songwriter and was quickly signed by Universal Music Publishing in Nashville (Brentwood-Benson Music Publishing/Universal CMG), where he has some 200 songs in his catalog. In 2010, he founded his publishing company, Great British Music, which now represents his work.

Simon's songs have been recorded by Vince Gill and Sheri Easter ("Livin' in the Rain"), American Idol finalist Mandisa

("Truth About Me"), Abandon ("Known"), Avalon ("Destined"), Gold City ("Never Too Broken") and many others in a range of genres.

"Livin' in the Rain" reached #2 on the SoGo charts and was long-listed for a Grammy. In 2012, Mandisa's album "What If We Were Real," which included "Truth About Me," was nominated for a Grammy. "Never Too Broken" reached #1 on the SoGo charts in autumn 2014. Simon also received a Dove nomination for the musical LifeSong: The Musical, written with Sue C Smith.

In 2015, Simon's modern hymn "He Is God" won the Integrity Music "Search for a Hymn 2015" competition, which he recorded with Integrity/Thankyou Music.

Simon's book *Song Maps - A New System to Write Your Best Lyrics* is still a #1 best seller on Amazon, internationally.

Simon is on the faculty of Write About Jesus, an annual conference based in St Louis, Missouri, that aims to equip and inspire Christian songwriters. He is also part of Harbour Creative, an HTB church plant in Portsmouth, England.

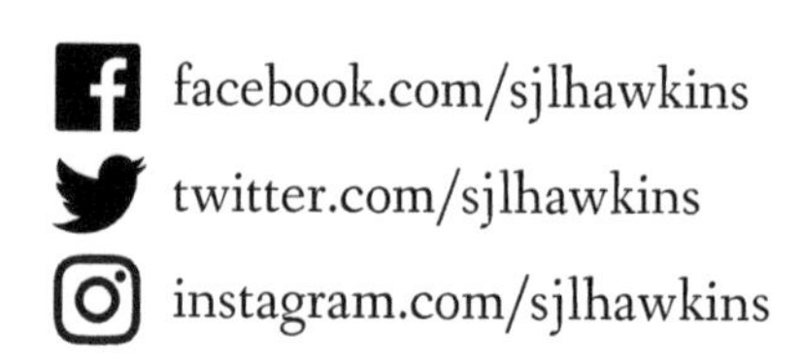

ALSO BY SIMON HAWKINS

The Organized Songwriter — How to Create Space to Write Your Best Songs

The Organized Songwriter Workbook

Song Maps — A New System to Write Your Best Lyrics

Song Maps Workbook